CONSUMER DURABLES AND INSTALLMENT DEBT:
a study of american households

by Gary Hendricks
and Kenwood C. Youmans,
with Janet Keller

Survey Research Center
Institute for Social Research
The University of Michigan

ISR Code No. 3304

Library of Congress Catalog Card No. 72-619719
ISBN 0-87944-117-8 paperbound
ISBN 0-87944-138-0 clothbound

Published by the Institute for Social Research
The University of Michigan, Ann Arbor, Mich. 48106

Contents

Preface

The analysis in this volume focuses on two major and related aspects of consumer behavior: expenditures on major consumer durable goods and the use of installment credit. The shorter-run dynamics of expenditure and installment debt behavior are alluded to from time to time, but the major emphasis is upon the longer-run trends of these two important financial characteristics of households, the important relations which underlie these trends, and the factors which have altered and may continue to alter these basic relationships.

In early 1967, the Survey Research Center interviewed a national cross section of 2,604 primary family units whose heads were under age 60. The interviews were repeated each year, with the final interview early in 1970. Extensive questions were asked regarding the income of the family during the previous year, the major purchases the family had made, and the amount of the family's outstanding installment debt. The extent of the family's holdings in financial assets was ascertained, as were the current level of major financial commitments held at the time of each interview. Extensive data were gathered on the attitudes of the family toward the use of various financial instruments—particularly installment debt—the level of the family's satisfaction with its current level of assets, and the family's subjective analysis of its past financial progress and future financial prospects.

Of the 2,604 families who completed the first interview, 1,921 were located for a second interview in 1968, 1,579 families responded to the third, and at the fourth round a panel of 1,436 of the original 2,604 families remained.

There are a number of published studies of expenditures on consumer durables, and most of them have examined one or more of the relationships examined here. Therefore, the part of this study devoted to expenditure is less unique for the relationships it considers than for the panel estimates of these relationships. The primary advantages are that (1) variables such as income change can be introduced directly into the analysis. For example, one need not assume that families whose circumstances are recently changed will behave similarly to those who attained a similar status quite some time ago. (2) By using averages over longer periods, the analyst avoids the effects of transitory phenomena which may bias estimates of cross section relations and obscure the effects of some variables in estimates based upon single cross sections.

Studies of installment debt are less common than studies of expenditures on major consumer durables. This study investigates attitudes toward debt, the relation of these attitudes to installment debt use, and possible association between growth in consumer installment credit over time and changing attitudes toward debt.

In addition to the data from the panel, the analysis of this volume takes advantage of the wealth of annual cross-section data available from the past 20 years of the Surveys of Consumer Finances whenever this is possible and seems useful in clarifying issues important to the analysis.

In addition to this volume, there are a number of earlier works which use data collected in the first two and three years of the SRC consumer panel.

Brief studies of the variability from one year to the next of family income, expenditures on major durables, outstanding installment debt balances and liquid assets appeared as separate chapters in the *1968* and *1969 Annual Survey of Consumer Finances* monographs. [1] Also appearing in the *1968 Survey of Consumer Finances* is a chapter which deals with the proportion of families who experience difficulties in meeting their installment debt obligations and with the characteristics of these families. The findings of these earlier reports are not reproduced in this volume. A study using data from the first two waves of the panel considers adjustments in installment debt balances within the framework of a stock adjustment model and appears in *The American Economic Review*.[2] These studies, as well as the current one, are useful introductions to the data available in the panel and the wide range of uses to which the data are applicable.

Those who may wish to use the panel to explore other problems or other aspects of problems already treated will want to peruse Appendix D, where the final composition of the panel is discussed in detail. A brief note on the time structure of the data and a sample of one of the four panel questionnaires is reproduced as Appendix E. Requests for the data tape and codebook documentation should be addressed to Ms. Evelyn Hansmire, The Institute for Social Research, Ann Arbor, Michigan, 48106.

---

[1] Copies of these volumes are available from Order Fulfillment Section, Institute for Social Research, The University of Michigan, Ann Arbor, Michigan, 48106.

[2] William C. Dunkelberg and Frank P. Stafford, "Debt in the Consumer Portfolio: Evidence from a Panel Study," *The American Economic Review*, September, 1971.

Acknowledgements

Any study whose design and completion spans almost five years is indebted to a large number of people. The authors are especially indebted to their colleague and teacher, Professor George Katona, who offered invaluable advice and consultation at all stages of the research and actively participated in the writing of several chapters. A special debt is also owed to our colleague James N. Morgan for his reading of the final draft and his assistance in getting it published.

The collection and preparation of the data was a joint effort of many at the Survey Research Center. George Katona and James N. Morgan shared the custodial responsibility for the progress and completion of the data collection and this report. In addition to their work on the Surveys of Consumer Finances, William Dunkelberg and Frank P. Stafford participated in the design of the panel and directed the first three years of data collection. The original sample selection was the responsibility of the Sampling Section of the Survey Research Center, directed by Irene Hess. The field work was carried out by the Field Section of the Center under the direction of John Scott. The many editing, coding and re-editing operations were done by the permanent coding staff of the Survey Research Center under the direction of Joan Scheffler.

In addition to her direct contribution to this volume, Janet Keller deserves special recognition for her careful supervision and coordination of the various survey operations from the beginning of the data collection in early 1967 to the final documentation and archiving of the data in 1971. Her painstaking efforts have undoubtedly greatly increased the quality of the final data set and its usefulness to those outside the Center. Finally, we would like to thank our many friends at the Survey Research Center who aided in both large and small ways in the completion and preparation of the manuscript, and Priscilla Hildebrandt who typed the tabular material which appears in this volume. We acknowledge the editorial help of Bill Haney, Linda Stafford, and Douglas Truax in directing the publishing of the manuscript.

The data collection and analysis for this report were financed by a grant from the Ford Foundation. We gratefully acknowledge the Foundation's support.

Chapter 1

INTRODUCTION

During the 1930's and immediately following World War II, economic growth and stability occupied the limelight of social concern. In the 1960's and now in the early 1970's other pressing social and economic issues have moved to the fore and vie for the attention of both researchers and policy makers. However, the need to provide basic economic stability and to anticipate and plan for changes in economic trends is no less important today than it was 20 years ago. Indeed, economic stability may be requisite to the resolution of many of the social and economic issues which currently concern Americans.

No one study can consider all of the many dimensions of the problems of economic growth and stability. This study, like others, is very restricted. We examine here only issues related to expenditures on major durables and consumer installment debt. In examining these issues we have not tried to substantiate any particular theory. Neither has prediction been our primary goal. Rather we have tried to add to the understanding of the economic events and trends of the postwar period and have attempted to gain at least some insight into the factors which will influence the basic movements of these two important economic aggregates over the coming decade.

In carrying out our objective we have focused on a limited set of long-run cross-section relations. We examine the differences in average levels of expenditures on major consumer durables and average holdings of installment debt of families of different socio-economic status, with divergent financial experiences over the four years between 1966 and 1971 and holding divergent attitudes regarding the desirability of using installment debt as a means of fulfilling their consumption objectives. The specific relations we examine are those which we believe have been important in determining past trends in the aggregate demand for consumer durables and consumer installment debt or which will be important in explaining future movements in these aggregates.

In this introduction we define the two major dependent variables toward

3

which our attention is directed. We then review briefly the postwar trends which the analysis is designed to help explain, and finally we describe the logical structure of the study.

Defining Outlays on Major Durables

In this study expenditures on major durable goods are defined as reported outlays, minus proceeds from trade-ins and related sales, on automobiles and major household durables. As in the annual Surveys of Consumer Finances, "automobiles" indicate privately owned passenger cars. Trucks, although they may be used as personal transportation, are excluded, as are motor bikes, scooters, and motorcycles. Major household durables include all major appliances and smaller appliances such as sewing machines, vacuum cleaners and air conditioners.

Past studies of expenditures on major durables have often included additions and repairs to the home. We have not included them here. Owners and renters both make choices about the level of maintenance for which they are willing to pay. Owners pay this cost directly, while for renters the cost is included in a rental payment. Similarly, while owners have the option of adding to their homes in order to adjust their stock of housing, renters seldom have this option and usually make adjustments by moving to another unit.[1] Thus the inclusion of this variable is likely to produce an owner versus renter bias. Even among homeowners, including additions and repairs in the major expenditures variable will tend to introduce unwanted variance since adjustments in housing by buying a new house are not included.

Housing purchases are, of course, not included in durable expenditures as defined here. Housing purchases entail a much more extensive commitment of resources over a much longer period of time than do the purchases of other major durables. The factors which influence these decisions are different than for other durables. Moreover, the transactions in buying and selling houses involve rather substantial costs, and adjustments are not affected by the small and often nonpersisting changes in income observed over one or two years. Even with four years of data, one cannot be sure that a family, even with a rather substantial change in income, would have had enough time or incentive to adjust its housing.

Finally, an expenditure variable was constructed by summing the prices paid minus the value of any trade-ins or related sales for all reported purchases of automobiles and major household durables made by the family be-

---

[1]A similar though less extreme problem arises for renters who rent furnished housing units. It should be noted that less than 20 percent of renters report renting furnished quarters, however, and that appliances such as stoves, refrigerators and other built in durables are often included in the price of the house for homeowners. To the extent that some expenditures for durables are hidden in housing payments, survey estimates of the demand for household durables will understate the true demand originating in the household sector.

tween January of 1966 and the end of December of 1969. This total was then divided by four to obtain an estimate of annual average expenditures for the family. Throughout this volume, when we speak of families having expenditures of so many dollars per year, we are referring to this four-year annual average.

Measuring Installment Debt

Installment debt is defined in this study as all private, non-mortgage debt of the household which is subject to three or more regular payments regardless of timing. Thirty-day charge accounts and transactions in which the purchaser promised to pay within 30 days are not included, but revolving charges are. Installment debt incurred on car or durable purchases is included, as is non-mortgage installment debt related to house additions and repair expenses, loans for other major transactions when specific items were mentioned, and loans to consolidate debt. Current bills and debts related to investments to make money or to real estate that the family is not personally using are excluded, as are all other business-related debts.

Although the data do permit classification of debt by purpose for which the debt was incurred (auto debt, debt on household durables, other personal debt), no such distinction is made here. Regardless of the reason for incurring the debt, once incurred the implications of having debt for the future behavior of the family are likely to be the same.

The use of installment debt has several dimensions and can be measured in a number of ways. Here we define it as the amount of outstanding debt owed by the family on the day on which the family was interviewed. To obtain a measure of total outstanding installment debt, we asked families the size of the monthly payment for each separate loan and the number of installments left to pay. The amount outstanding on each loan was calculated by multiplying the amount of the monthly payment by the number of payments left, taking account of any difference in the size of the last payment to be made. The results were summed for all loans for each family. For the analysis of this volume an estimate of average outstanding installment balances is employed. This estimate was obtained by summing the total of outstanding installment debt at the time of each of the four interviews and dividing that total by four.

Postwar Trends.

The interest in economic studies is not in what they can tell us about the present, but in how they can help to explain the past and to understand what may happen in the future. Since the original intent of the analysis was to add to our understanding of the events of the postwar period, we have summarized in Table 1-1 the aggregate trends in personal disposable income, expenditures on major durables and end of year consumer installment

Table 1-1

AGGREGATE TRENDS IN DISPOSABLE INCOME, EXPENDITURES ON CONSUMER
DURABLES AND CONSUMER INSTALLMENT CREDIT, 1950-1970

(Billions of Dollars)

Year	Disposable Personal Income	Personal Expenditures on Major Durables[1]	Ratio of Expenditures on Major Durables to Disposable Income[2]	Total Outstanding Consumer Installment Credit[3]	Ratio of Outstanding Installment Credit to Disposable Income[4]
1950	206.9	27.2	13.1	14.7	7.1
1951	226.6	26.0	11.5	15.3	6.7
1952	238.3	25.4	10.7	19.4	8.1
1953	252.6	29.1	11.5	23.0	9.1
1954	257.4	28.6	11.1	23.6	9.2
1955	275.3	35.0	12.7	28.9	10.5
1956	293.2	33.9	11.6	31.7	10.8
1957	308.5	35.6	11.5	33.9	11.0
1958	318.8	32.5	10.2	33.6	10.5
1959	337.3	38.4	11.4	39.2	11.6
1960	350.0	39.0	11.1	43.0	12.3
1961	364.4	37.7	10.3	43.9	12.0
1962	385.3	42.5	11.0	48.7	12.6
1963	404.6	46.5	11.5	55.5	13.7
1964	438.1	50.8	11.6	62.7	14.3
1965	473.2	57.2	12.1	71.3	15.1
1966	511.9	60.2	11.8	77.5	15.1
1967	546.3	61.9	11.3	80.9	14.8
1968	591.0	71.8	12.1	89.9	15.2
1969	634.2	76.7	12.1	98.2	15.5
1970	687.8	74.5	10.8	101.2	14.7

Source: Economic Report of the President, January, 1972.

[1] Includes personal consumption expenditures on automobiles and parts and on furniture and household equipment.

[2] Ratio of column (2) to column (1). Ratios are in percent.

[3] End of year outstanding balances.

[4] Ratio of column (4) to column (1). Ratios are in percent.

debt balances from 1950 through 1970. The figures in Table 1-1 are in current dollars and the ratios shown are in percent.

With only minor exceptions a steady upward trend in personal disposable income both in constant and in real dollars has characterized the postwar period. Accompanying this growth has been a steady increase in expenditures on automobiles and other major household durables. However, these increased expenditures represent about the same proportion of personal disposable income. In the period 1950-1954, expenditures on automobiles, furniture and other household equipment were a little over 11 percent of disposable personal income. Fifteen years later expenditures on these durables were still a little over 11 percent of disposable personal income. While there has been no significant change in the portion of disposable personal income being spent on consumer durables, the year-to-year volatility of purchases of these goods, which is evident in Table 1-1, makes them one of the most interesting and important components of gross national product.[2]

In contrast to expenditures on major consumer durables which have remained stable as a proportion of income, outstanding installment debt balances have tended to increase at a much faster rate than income. While expenditures on cars and other major household equipment has almost tripled, aggregate installment debt outstanding—a substantial proportion of which is specifically related to purchases of consumer durables—has increased sevenfold from about $15 billion in 1950 to almost $110 billion at the end of 1970. The steady increase in installment debt and the ratio of installment debt to personal income has continued throughout the 20-year period almost without interruption.

Organization of the Study

The study begins in Chapter 2 with an analysis of the impact of income on expenditures for major durables. In this analysis the panel is utilized by relating average annual expenditure levels to average annual income. Using averages over several years eliminates the problem of limited dependent variables, which is encountered with single surveys in which data for the most recent year are all that can be collected due to memory bias. In addition, extending the accounting period to four years alleviates to some extent the bias in survey relationships which arises because of errors in independent variables and, in particular, irregularities in income.

Chapter 2 also considers the relation of installment debt balances to aver-

---

[2]For a more complete discussion of fluctuations in household capital formation and the growth of household capital relative to fixed business capital, see F. Thomas Juster, *Household Capital Formation and Financing, 1867-1962* National Bureau of Economics Research, 1966. Juster also discusses the growth of consumer installment credit.

age income level for families in the panel. The stability over time of the relation of installment debt to income is examined using data from the annual Surveys of Consumer Finances dating back to 1955.

In Chapter 2 three questions are raised: (1) What accounts for the variance in expenditures and installment debt left unexplained by income? (2) How stable have the relations of installment debt and expenditures to income been in the past and can we expect them to be stable in the future? and (3) To what extent do the cross-section relations reflect only the impact of income on expenditures and installment debt, and to what extent do they reflect other characteristics of families that happen to be correlated with income?

In Chapter 3 we digress briefly to compare the distributions of the variables of Chapter 2 for a single year and for longer accounting periods. Some preliminary comments are made regarding the extent to which important independent variables may be obscured by one-year data where there are severe problems of measurement error in the independent variables and where dependent variables are limited in nature. Parts of the analysis of Chapter 2 are reproduced using only a single year's data from the panel.

In Chapter 4 we return to the issues raised in Chapter 2. Chapter 4 examines the relation of demographic characteristics other than income to expenditures on consumer durables and installment debt use. This chapter also attempts to evaluate how these characteristics influence the relationships observed between income and expenditures and income and installment debt. Particular attention is paid here to family life cycle, its various components, and to housing status.

In drawing inferences about the behavior of families in a typical cross-section sample, one of the major problems is the necessity to group together all members of a status group regardless of whether these members are new entrants into that status group or are persons who have held that status for some time. In Chapter 5 we take advantage of the reinterview structure of the panel to calculate income trend and income variance measures for each individual family. These trends are then related to expenditure levels and expenditure rates in order to discover the extent to which income changes may lead to accelerated rates of expenditures and hence stimulate accelerated economic growth and inflationary pressure. The impact of income trends on average installment debt balances is also examined.

Income trends and the variance around these trends are only two of the many dimensions of income change. Chapter 6 considers yet another dimension: perceptions of changes and expectations regarding future changes. Perception of changes in financial well-being and future income expectations have been discussed in a large number of contexts both in the theoretical and the empirical literature. In Chapter 6 we examine a cumulative measure of one-year perceptions of change over the past year and expectations regarding the coming year.

In Chapter 7 attitudes toward the use of installment debt are related to levels of outstanding installment debt. The stability of these measures for the same families in successive years of the panel is examined and changes in attitudes as well as levels are related to average installment debt balances. Data from earlier studies conducted by the Survey Research Center are used to examine the trend in these attitudes over time and the possible relation of these attitudes to shifts in the installment debt-to-income relation of Chapter 2.

The final chapter of this volume summarizes the findings of the individual chapters and makes some recommendations for further research using the panel data on which most of the discussion of this report is based.

Chapter 2

MAJOR EXPENDITURES, INSTALLMENT DEBT AND INCOME

Any study of expenditures on major durables and installment debt must have as its starting point the relation of these two important financial variables to income. Income is without question the most important single determinant of expenditures on major consumer durables and is an important predictor of the use of installment credit as well. A thorough understanding of the relation between income and expenditures on major durables by households and the use of installment debt is, therefore, requisite in explaining past movements in financial aggregates and predicting movements in the future. Moreover, knowledge of the impact of income is essential (1) to gaining an understanding of the way in which other factors, many of which are correlated with income, may affect expenditures and debt use, and (2) to sorting out the relative importance of these factors.

Measuring Income

Annual measures of the total income of the family were ascertained from an extensive series of questions which asked specifically about the income received by each individual family member and from each of an extensive list of sources. The questions, reproduced in the questionnaire in Appendix E, parallel those developed and used in the annual Surveys of Consumer Finances. On the basis of the information on income received from various sources and accruing to each member of the family, the appropriate filing units for the family were determined and federal income tax liabilities were estimated separately for each unit. The tax liabilities across all filing units in the family were then summed and subtracted from the total income of the family. No adjustments were made for tax liabilities other than federal income taxes. Throughout this volume annual income refers to total family income after the deduction of estimated federal income tax liabilities.

Since our primary interest is in the longer-run relationships between expenditures, installment debt and their various determinants, and in possible shifts in these relations over time, income was averaged over the four years of the panel by summing income across the four individual years and dividing by four.

Using average annual income minimizes the bias which ordinarily arises in estimating cross-section relations with a single year's income. [1]

The Relation of Expenditures to Income

On average, families in the panel spent slightly more than 8 percent of their income over four years on automobiles and major household durables. Since the national accounts data include a somewhat larger set of items than our measure of consumer durable goods and since aggregate disposable income excludes more tax liabilities than our measure of income, the panel average compares favorably with the 11.8 percent estimate of the proportion of income spent on consumer durables obtained for the same period from the national accounts data shown in Table 1-1.

The dollar amounts families spend on cars and household durables increase steadily as income rises. As shown in Table 2-1, each successively higher income group spends substantially more than the group immediately below it. [2] Families with an income of less than $3,000 spent only slightly more than $100 per year for the maintenance and expansion of their inventories of durables; families with an income between $8,500 and $10,000—the group in which falls the mean income for the panel—spent about $830 per year; and families with an income of $15,000 or more spent, on the average, $1,200 or more each year on major consumer durables.

While amounts spent increase steadily with income, the proportion of income invested in consumer durables is not the same at all income levels. Families in the panel with average incomes of less than $5,000 per year spent

---

[1] The problem of errors in variables is well-known. Its probable impact on consumption and saving relationships with income is discussed extensively by Milton Friedman in *A Theory of the Consumption Function,* National Bureau of Economic Research, Number 63, General Series, 1957. A general discussion of the problem of errors in variables and its impact on relationships in the generalized least squares model appears in *Econometric Methods* by J. Johnson (1963), Chapter 6.

[2] Of the 1,436 families who completed all four of the panel interviews, 30 families had expenditure-to-income ratios over four years equalling or exceeding 25 percent of their incomes. Since a few extreme cases may have a very large impact on the mean of a subgroup, these 30 families are not included in the tabulations of Table 2-1. These families are also excluded from other tabulations involving expenditures on cars and major household durables unless noted otherwise. The characteristics of the 30 families who spent 25 percent or more of their incomes on cars and major household durables are discussed in Appendix C.

Table 2-1

EXPENDITURES ON MAJOR DURABLES AND THE RATIO OF EXPENDITURES TO INCOME
BY FOUR-YEAR AVERAGE ANNUAL INCOME
(Class Means and Standard Deviations)

Four-Year Average Income	Four-Year Average Expenditure	One Standard Deviation	Ratio of Expenditures to Income	One Standard Deviation	Proportion of Families	Number of Families
Less than $3,000	120	129	5.6	5.7	6	81
$3,000-4,999	266	239	6.5	5.9	8	110
$5,000-5,999	499	356	9.1	6.6	8	110
$6,000-7,499	655	405	9.5	5.9	14	195
$7,500-8,499	734	444	9.1	5.6	12	166
$8,500-9,999	829	513	8.9	5.5	15	211
$10,000-12,499	989	576	8.8	5.1	18	250
$12,500-14,999	1176	591	8.6	4.3	9	133
$15,000-19,999	1238	708	7.4	4.3	6	87
$20,000 or more	1752	918	6.7	4.0	4	63
All families	811	626	8.4	5.5	100	1406

NOTE: Four-year average expenditure is measured in dollars per year. The ratios of expenditures to income are percents.

only about 6 percent of their income on consumer durables. As income rises above the $5,000 per year level, however, the proportion of income allocated to investments in automobiles and large household items rises to 9 percent. Roughly speaking, the fraction of income allocated to purchases of cars and major household durables remains constant over the whole middle range of the income distribution. Families whose average annual incomes were as divergent as $5,000 and $15,000 all spend an average of about 9 percent of their income after federal income taxes on major durables. About 75 percent of all panel families, and probably a fairly similar proportion of families in the total population, had annual incomes between $5,000 and $15,000 a year over the period 1966-1969.

Although care must be taken not to attribute too much significance to small differences in expenditure rates, the data in Table 2-1 strongly suggest that even among middle income families average expenditure rates differ between the lower-middle and upper-middle income segments of the middle income group. For the panel families, expenditure rates on major durables reach a peak at an income level between $6,000 and $7,500 and thereafter begin to decline. The decline is slow at first but accelerates markedly at income levels of $15,000 or more, becoming less than 8 percent for the group of families with an income between $15,000 and $20,000 per year, and less than 7 percent for families with an income above $20,000. Families with very substantial amounts of discretionary spending power, like those with very limited amounts, spend proportionately less than middle income families on conventional durable goods.

For purposes of prediction and projection, it is often convenient to summarize relations in a more concise form than in Table 2-1. The method most frequently employed is least squares regressions which are concise and yield simple summary estimates of the responsiveness of the dependent variable to one or more independent variables.

As a first approximation we fit the simple least squares regression most often used in the past to summarize the relation of expenditures on major durables to income. Simply regressing average expenditures per year (E) for each family on average annual income (Y) yields the following:

(1) $E = 283 + .054 Y$
     (22.3) $R^2 = .262$

where R^2 is the proportion of variance in expenditures explained adjusted for degrees of freedom and the number shown in parentheses below the slope coefficient on income is a t-ratio.[3]

---

[3]A t-ratio is obtained by dividing the standard error of a coefficient into the coefficient itself. Hence for the regression shown above the t-ratio of 22.3 indicates that the coefficient on four-year average annual income is 22.3 times its standard error. For a simple random sample the size

As expected, while Table 2-1 clearly indicates that expenditures on major durables are quite responsive to differences in income level over a broad range of income, indeed, among all income groups except those in the top 10 percent of the distribution, regression (1) indicates that expenditures on major durables change only very moderately in response to differences in income level. According to the slope coefficient on income, an increase in annual income of $1,000 will lead to an average annual increase in investments in consumer durables of only slightly more than $50.

If we wanted to predict the response of aggregate expenditures on major consumer durables as total personal income rose over time on the basis of equation (1), we could do so by calculating the income elasticity of the demand for durables from the equation. An elasticity is defined as the ratio of a percentage change in one variable to a percentage change in another. In the case of expenditures and income, this would be the ratio of the percentage change in expenditures on consumer durables that would result from a one percent change in income.

Since the elasticity of a linear function which does not pass through the origin is not constant, we evaluate the income elasticity of the demand for consumer durables at the mean of average annual income and expenditures. In the case of equation (1) above, the elasticity of expenditures with respect to income is .65—the slope of the regression line (.054) times the ratio of mean income to mean expenditures ($9731/$811)—indicating that, as mean income rises, the proportion of income spent on consumer durables will fall. Moreover, on the basis only of equation (1), as income continues to rise the elasticity of expenditures associated with further income increases will fall to even less than .65.

The finding that expenditures on major durables or even total expenditures appear unresponsive to income changes when a regression is used to summarize the cross-section expenditure-income relation is not new. In fact, it is widely known that cross-section data consistently yield much lower estimates than time series data of the responsiveness of expenditures on consumer durables to changes in income.[4]

We suggest that one problem is that too often very little attention and thought is given to the underlying distributions prior to regression analysis and the estimation of elasticities. In using regression (1) to summarize the re-

---

of our sample, a t-ratio of 1.6 is sufficient for statistical significance at a 90 percent level of confidence. The panel is not a simple random sample, however, and our own preference is that coefficients be at least twice as large as their standard errors and preferably three times as large before they are considered highly significant. For a discussion of the sampling errors of complex statistics from non-simple random samples see Martin R. Frankel, *Inference From Survey Samples: An Empirical Investigation*. Institute for Social Research, Ann Arbor, Michigan, 1971.

[4]The inconsistency between times-series and cross-section estimates applies not only to expenditures on consumer durables but also to housing and almost all other commodity groups including total expenditures.

lation of expenditures to income, we assume that the relation between income and investments in major durables is a linear one. In Graph 2-1, mean four-year average annual expenditures on automobiles plus major household durables are plotted by family income. Casual inspection of Graph 2-1 is adequate evidence that to assume a linear relation for purposes of estimating the possible responsiveness of purchases of major durables to the longer-run general trend in income is likely to bias substantially downward the estimate of the responsiveness of expenditures to income.

Deriving an appropriate mathematical function to describe the relation shown in Graph 2-1 is difficult. However, since our expectation is that the trend in income will be upward, we have looked for a functional form that takes into account the declining proportion of income allocated to expenditures on major durables as incomes rise above $7,500 rather than one which takes account very precisely of the rise in the proportion of income spent on durables at the lower income end of the income distribution. Our strategy is clearly a compromise, but it seems better than ignoring the non-linearity entirely.

The best fit found for the relationship was obtained by using a regression which included both four-year average income (Y) and a parabolic term, four-year average income squared (Y^2). The estimated relationship is as follows:

$$(2) \quad E = -37 + .105 \ Y - .00000131 \ Y^2$$
$$\quad \quad \quad \quad (20.8) \quad \quad (11.3) \quad \quad \quad \quad \quad \quad \quad R^2 = .324$$

The regression which includes the non-linear term Y^2, not only fits the data better, as indicated by the increase in the proportion of variance in expenditures explained, but more importantly, the results conform much more closely to the expenditure-income relation suggested by aggregate trends over the postwar period.

On the basis of the postwar historical experience, one would expect that the proportion of income allocated to expenditures on major durables would approximate a ray through the origin and that the coefficient on income would be approximately equal to the average proportion of income allocated to expenditures. In fact, the constant term in equation (2) is not very different from zero, and the slope of the relation with income is quite close to the proportion of income actually allocated to purchases of major durables.

While the results of equation (2) conform much more closely to the actual postwar experience, this is not entirely the case. As pointed out earlier, the proportion of total disposable income invested in major nonhousing durables by consumers has remained constant, except for cyclical variation, over the entire postwar period. On the basis solely of the evidence provided by equation (2), we would expect this to be only approximately true. Estimating the

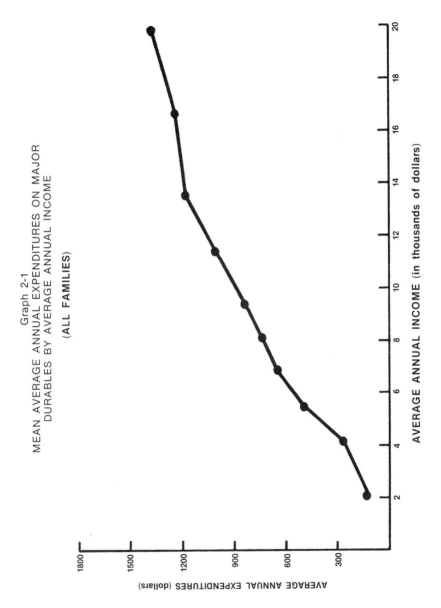

Graph 2-1
MEAN AVERAGE ANNUAL EXPENDITURES ON MAJOR
DURABLES BY AVERAGE ANNUAL INCOME

(ALL FAMILIES)

average annual investment in cars and household durables implied by equation (2) at the mean of income for the panel, and calculating the income elasticity at that point on the fitted expenditure function, yields an estimate of .90. While this estimate of the income elasticity of the demand for durables is substantially higher than that obtained from the simple linear formulation of the expenditure function, it still falls short of the estimate of 1.0 implied by a casual perusal of the postwar time-studies data. The difference, however, is not difficult to reconcile.

An elasticity is a highly simplistic and concise way to summarize data and in the case of equation (2) is not constant over the entire range of income. At incomes below $10,000 the elasticity implied by equation (2) is very close to 1.0 and falls as income rises. Since real income has risen substantially since the war, we would expect that the demand for durables would have been very close to 1.0 over much of the period. Moreover, equation (2) does not take into account the fact that at lower income levels the elasticity of demand for cars and household durables exceeds one. Hence, if income increases were more or less evenly distributed among income groups, then families at lower incomes could have offset the declines in the proportion of income spent by families whose initial incomes were higher and were moving rapidly upward.

There is yet another reason to expect that investments in consumer durables might not have shown any tendency to fall relative to income over the postwar period. Throughout the postwar period consumer durables have become less expensive relative to the other goods which consumers purchase. This was especially true during the 1960's when, despite consistent increases in the prices of other categories of goods, the prices of durables rose hardly at all. Assuming that differences in the rate at which the price of durables rose relative to other commodities made durables more attractive, this would tend to shift the expenditure-income function for durables upward and hence increase the demand for durables at all levels of income.[5]

Although the postwar trends can easily be reconciled using the durables expenditure-income function summarized in Table 2-1 and equation (2), we cannot really escape the longer-run implications of the data. These data

----

[5]It is, of course, not necessarily true that a change in relative prices favorable to consumer durables will shift the expenditure-income function upward. There are income as well as substitution effects and the pattern of these two opposing forces may be quite complex. Habitual consumption patterns for everyday items are likely to adjust to changes in prices with some considerable lag. Moreover, it has been shown that many consumers resent rapid price increases, especially for goods such as foodstuffs, and in the short run, expenditures on major durables may fall when the prices of other goods rise noticeably. Over longer periods and when real incomes are rising, however, it seems likely that, since major consumer durables are an important part of the life style of many Americans, the overall impact of declines in the relative price would lead to increased spending on these items and to an upward shift in the durables expenditures-income function.

clearly suggest that Americans view conventional consumer durables not primarily as luxury items, but rather as necessities. Over a wide range of incomes the consumption of these durables, as reflected in average annual expenditures on them, increases almost in proportion to income. At relatively high incomes, however, the demand for durables expands less rapidly than income suggesting that at high levels of income additional dollars are diverted to expenditures on other types of consumption.[6]

If we interpret these data literally, we must predict that in the not too distant future expenditures on durables will grow more slowly than in the past and expenditures on these items will fall as a proportion of disposable personal income unless other factors which might compensate for this decline change. The legitimacy of transferring information derived from static cross-section relations at a point in time to changes which might occur over time, however, requires understanding what underlies the cross-section relations and to what extent these underlying factors are likely to remain constant.

Older families who are likely to have retired family heads and among whom the life cycle effect would be strongest are explicitly excluded from the panel. Thus, family life cycle and its close relation with earnings cycles which might be expected to be strong factors affecting the income-expenditure patterns when all population groups are considered, may not in fact be nearly so important among the panel families. The impact of life cycle differences on cross-section income-expenditure relationships is discussed in Chapter 4.

The Relation of Installment Debt Balances to Income

The pattern of average levels of outstanding debt across income groups differs markedly from the pattern of expenditures on consumer durables. Although the proportionate relationship with income declines in both cases, the decline is much more pronounced in the case of installment debt balances.

As shown in Table 2-2, not only does the proportion of outstanding installment debt begin to decline at incomes of $10,000 or more but at high incomes the absolute amount of installment debt declines as well. Families with an in-

---

[6]Although data on financial assets was gathered from the families in the panel, the relation between financial savings and income is not considered in this volume. It is wrong to assume, however, that the decline in expenditures on automobiles and major household durables at high incomes necessarily implies higher rates of financial savings. For example, questions were asked regarding expenditures on large recreation items and for vacations of five days or more in the last three years of the panel. Expanding the definition of major expenditures to include expenditures on large hobby and recreation items and vacations reduces substantially the differences between middle and higher income families in the proportion of their income spent on major discretionary items. For each of the income groups shown in Table 2-1 between $6,000 and $19,999, the ratio of "all" discretionary expenditures to income is between 11.0 and 11.7 percent. The ratio is 10.2 percent for families with incomes of $20,000 or more per year.

come of between $10,000 and $15,000 maintained debt balances of over $1,200, the highest balances in terms of absolute dollars, while families with an income between $15,000 and $20,000 and families with an income of $20,000 or more maintained lower dollar balances.

As found in past studies, the highest average ratios of outstanding installment debt are maintained by middle income families. These were families in the panel with an income between $5,000 and $10,000. In Table 2-2 middle income families are subdivided into several smaller income groups within income ranges of $1,000 to $1,500. For none of these groups does the average installment debt to income ratio vary by more than a few tenths of a percentage point from 12.0. The similarity of debt-to-income ratios in the middle income range, which includes approximately 50 percent of the families in the panel, suggests that despite large differences in family circumstances and the amount of debt which different families may feel comfortable carrying, there is some considerable agreement about what are appropriate levels of installment debt.

Contrary to much popular mythology, low income families are generally rather cautious in their use of installment debt, and on average maintain installment debt balances that are a smaller fraction of their income than do middle income families.[7] Despite the broad definition of installment debt, which includes debt incurred on purchases regardless of type, the 6 percent of families in the panel with average incomes of less than $3,000 per year maintained average installment debt balances equal to only 4 percent of their annual income, while allocating on average about 6 percent of their income to expenditures on automobiles and major household durables. This finding is more impressive when it is recalled that families with heads over age 59 in early 1967 were excluded from the panel.

As average income rises above $10,000, the ratio of installment debt balances to income declines markedly from the stable 12 percent ratio observed among families with an income between $5,000 and $10,000. For families with an income of $15,000 to $20,000 the ratio is only about two-thirds as high as for middle income families and for families with an income of $20,000 or more the ratio is only one-third as high (3.2 percent).

The lower ratio of installment debt balances to income among very low and relatively high income families may result either from fewer of these families using installment credit or from less credit being used by those who do use it or by a combination of these factors. In Graph 2-2 installment debt-to-income ratios are plotted separately for all families and for families who had installment debt at some time during the panel.

The relation of the two lines in Graph 2-2 suggests that the decline in

---

[7]Difficulties with the repayment of installment debt are discussed in Chapter 9 of the *1968 Survey of Consumer Finances,* Institute for Social Research, 1969.

Table 2-2

FOUR-YEAR AVERAGE OUTSTANDING INSTALLMENT DEBT AND THE RATIO OF INSTALLMENT DEBT TO INCOME
BY FOUR-YEAR AVERAGE ANNUAL INCOME
(Class Means and Standard Deviations)

Four-Year Average Income	Four-Year Average Debt	One Standard Deviation	Ratio of Debt to Income	One Standard Deviation
Less than $3,000	99	166	4.3	6.8
$3,000–4,999	328	386	8.1	9.7
$5,000–5,999	659	608	12.0	11.1
$6,000–7,499	796	756	11.6	11.1
$7,500–8,499	963	838	11.9	10.4
$8,500–9,999	1140	939	12.3	10.1
$10,000–12,499	1229	1227	10.9	10.7
$12,500–14,999	1247	1302	9.2	9.7
$15,000–19,999	1137	1221	6.8	7.3
$20,000 or more	917	1563	3.2	4.4
All families	923	1035	10.0	10.2

NOTE: Four-year average outstanding installment debt is in dollars. The ratios of installment debt to income are percents. See Chapter 1 for the precise definition of average outstanding installment debt.

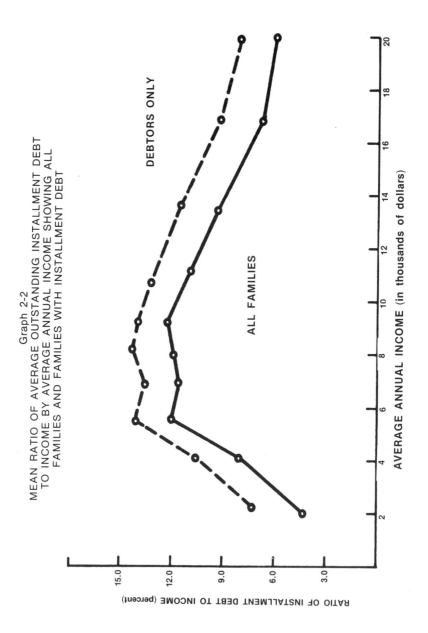

Graph 2-2

MEAN RATIO OF AVERAGE OUTSTANDING INSTALLMENT DEBT
TO INCOME BY AVERAGE ANNUAL INCOME SHOWING ALL
FAMILIES AND FAMILIES WITH INSTALLMENT DEBT

amounts of outstanding installment debt balances among higher income families is not simply the result of less frequent use of credit among these families. At the very ends of the distribution of income the gap between the two lines is slightly larger than elsewhere, indicating that a somewhat smaller percent of the families with an income of less than $3,000, or greater than $20,000 had any debt outstanding over the four years. However, the general finding is that even among installment debt users relatively low and relatively high income families tend to maintain lower average balances in relation to their incomes than do middle income families.[8]

The average installment debt balances maintained by families are not only a function of the amounts borrowed but also of the length of time taken to repay the debt and the cost of the borrowed funds. It is possible that the higher average balances of middle income people are not the result of financing a larger proportion of purchases with installment debt, but rather reflect longer repayment periods.

To test for this possibility, the ratio of the average of total monthly repayment obligations at the time of each of the four annual interviews to the average of outstanding installment debt was calculated for families who had debt in at least one of the four years. The ratios are shown below.

Average Annual Income	Ratio of Monthly Payments to Debt (Percent)
Less than $3,000	16.4
$3,000-4,999	11.1
$5,000-5,999	9.0
$6,000-7,499	8.6
$7,500-8,499	7.9
$8,500-9,999	7.4
$10,000-12,499	7.3
$12,500-14,999	8.0
$15,000-19,999	6.4
$20,000 or more	7.9
All Families	8.5

If average maturities were the same for each income group shown above, we would expect the ratio of total monthly payments to total debt outstanding would also be the same. Lower ratios of monthly payments to outstanding

---

[8]Nineteen percent of the families in the panel had no outstanding installment debt at the time of any of the four annual interviews. The characteristics of these non-installment debt users are discussed in Appendix B.

installment debt balances imply longer maturities, and higher ratios shorter maturities. [9]

For low and lower-middle income families the ratio of monthly payments to outstanding balances is clearly higher than for middle and upper income families. Thus, although families with modest incomes have lower average outstanding balances, they turn debt over more quickly. If it is true that debt use is no more seasonal for families with modest incomes than for middle income families, the data on average balances outstanding (Table 2-2) overstate the differences in debt use as a proportion of income between families with low incomes and middle income families.

According to Table 2-2, the use of installment debt begins to fall off at incomes of $10,000 and continues to fall as a proportion of income thereafter. The decline in outstanding debt balances at incomes over $10,000 does indeed seem to indicate a real decline in the use of installment credit. There is no indication in the tabulations above that maturities change substantially over this portion of the income distribution. Families with an average income of $20,000 or more who use installment debt do not pay off that debt at any faster rate than do families with an income between $7,500 and $8,500.

In short, the similarity of ratios of monthly payments to outstanding balances at all income levels above $7,500 is reassuring evidence that the relation of average installment debt balances (measured only once a year) to income is a fairly adequate gauge of the amount of installment credit families use. The data indicate that the leveling off of average installment debt balances at incomes of $10,000 a year or more reflects real differences in the amount of installment debt used by families with an income of under and over $10,000 and not just differences in maturities. The differences in outstanding debt balances between lower and middle income families, however, probably exaggerate the real differences in the amount of installment debt used.

Since there is such a sharp break in the installment debt function at incomes of $10,000 or more, it is difficult to derive a single, simple mathematical relation that accurately describes the use of installment debt over the entire income distribution. Therefore, separate estimates of the elasticity of installment debt balances with respect to income were obtained for families with an average income of less than $10,000 and families with an income of $10,000 or more. [10]

---

[9]The cost of borrowing does not enter into these calculations since it is included both in the monthly payments and in the measure of outstanding balances.

[10]Many economists would argue that the appropriate relation is not between income and installment debt balances but rather between installment debt balances and wealth. It seems to us, however, that the flow of income from wealth may be more important than wealth itself, especially since so much wealth is held in the form of human capital, and that the use of installment debt may be much less closely related to total wealth than to the form in which wealth is held. In any case, average income is probably a good proxy for wealth. Crude estimates of wealth

The regressions of average outstanding installment debt (D) on average annual income (Y) are shown below:

Income less than $10,000

$$(3) \quad D = -217 + .148 \ Y$$
$$ (13.5) \quad R^2 = .172$$

Income $10,000 or more

$$(4) \quad D = 1200 - .0012 \ Y$$
$$ (.145) \quad R^2 = .000$$

As expected, installment debt balances are responsive to changes in income for families with incomes of less than $10,000. Each additional $100 of income is associated with an increase in average installment debt balance of about $15. Although the coefficient on income is negative for the higher income group of families, it is not statistically significant with a t-ratio of substantially less than the 2.5 to 3.0 required to place any high degree of confidence in the coefficient on income being different from zero. The regression and Table 2-2 do suggest that, if there were enough very high income families in the panel, the income coefficient might be significantly negative for families with incomes of $10,000 or more.

At the mean income for families with an income of less than $10,000, the income elasticity of outstanding installment debt is 1.1, indicating that as income increases (or decreases) average outstanding installment increases (or decreases) almost in proportion to the change in income. At an income of $10,000 or more, installment debt balances are almost completely unresponsive to changes in income.

As indicated by the proportion of the variance in outstanding installment debt balances explained by income in the regressions above and by the standard deviations in Table 2-2, families with very similar incomes differ greatly in the amounts of installment debt they use.[11] Indeed, the standard deviations in Table 2-2 present a striking contrast to those for expenditures on major durables in Table 2-1. As in the case of expenditures, the variance in levels of outstanding installment debt increases with income and probably for many of the same reasons. However, in contrast to expenditures, where on the whole the amount of dispersion about the mean is much less, the standard deviations do not decline relative to average debt as income rises, but if anything increase, especially at income levels above $10,000 per year. Within income groups then, families are much more homogeneous with respect to the amounts they spend on major durables than they are with respect to the amounts they borrow and the length of time over which they repay their debts.

---

could be obtained for the panel since data are available on house values, mortgage debt, the value of car stocks and financial assets owned by the family.

[11] A part of this difference may reflect differences in maturities between families rather than in the amounts of debt incurred.

Changes in the Debt-Income Function Over Time

The sharp break in patterns of debt use at an income of $10,000 may have important implications for the future growth of the market in consumer installment credit. Much of the growth in installment debt during the 1950's and early 1960's was the result of the greater use of installment debt among relatively high income families. The aggregate trend data presented in Table 1-1 suggest that the rate of the upward shift in the debt-income function may have been declning during the latter half of the decade of the 1960's and that the relation between debt and income may possibly have stabilized now that installment debt is so widely available and widely accepted. If this is true, the data in Table 2-2 and the regressions of the last section imply that, as real income rises in the future, installment debt will rise less than in proportion to the change in income and at a much slower rate than over the past two decades.

To study the stability of the relation of debt and income over time, we use data from the 1956, 1960, 1965, and 1969 Surveys of Consumer Finances. The surveys were conducted each year by the Survey Research Center with a cross-section of American households. Work tables were assembled showing for each year the average amount of outstanding installment debt at different income levels. Since the change in price level over the 13 years is too large to ignore, incomes were deflated by the Consumer Price Index and graphs plotted for each year showing average outstanding installment debt by income, in constant 1957-59 dollars. From these graphs it is possible to read the estimated mean outstanding installment debt for different specific incomes. Since it was not possible to obtain data either on a family unit or on a spending unit basis for all years, the 1956 and 1960 statistics were derived from spending unit data and the 1965 and 1969 statistics were derived from family unit data.[12]

The results of this exercise are shown in Table 2-3 and Graph 2-3. For families with an income of less than $5,000 in 1957-1959 dollars, average levels of installment debt show no clear trend between 1956 and 1969. Except for individual year differences, the relation of debt to income has been stable throughout the last decade and a half for this income group. For families with an income greater than $5,000, however, there is a clear trend.

In 1960, spending units at any given level of income above $5,000 held larger amounts of outstanding installment debt than did spending units at that income level four years earlier, in 1956. For example, families with an income

---

[12]A family unit is defined as all persons living in the same dwelling unit who are related by blood, marriage or adoption. A single person unrelated to the other occupants in the dwelling unit or living alone is a family unit by himself. A spending unit is all related persons living together who pool their incomes. Husband, wife and children under age 18 living at home are always considered to be members of the same spending unit.

Table 2-3

MEAN DOLLAR AMOUNT OF OUTSTANDING INSTALLMENT DEBT
BY INCOME FOR SELECTED YEARS, 1956-1969

Income[2]	Year of Survey[1]			
	1956	1960	1965	1969
$1,000	75	100	60	85
$2,000	135	165	110	90
$3,000	230	270	255	250
$4,000	300	340	440	350
$5,000	425	445	500	590
$6,000	475	530	635	730
$7,000	475	535	685	815
$8,000	465	530	720	895
$9,000	460	530	725	965
$10,000	445	540	730	1020
$11,000	430	540	735	1000
$12,000	415	550	720	980
$13,000	400	560	705	960
$14,000	390	560	690	945
$15,000	380	570	670	925
$16,000	370	550	650	905
$17,000	360	525	635	890
$18,000	350	500	620	870
$19,000	340	480	600	850
$20,000	330	460	580	835

Source: Annual Surveys of Consumer Finances,
1956 through 1969.

[1]All surveys were taken during the first quarter of
the year shown.   Income is before taxes and is for
the calendar year prior to the year in which the
survey was taken.

[2]All income figures are in 1957-1959 dollars.

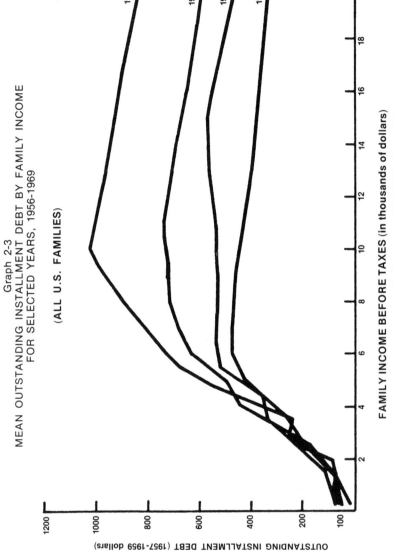

Graph 2-3
MEAN OUTSTANDING INSTALLMENT DEBT BY FAMILY INCOME
FOR SELECTED YEARS, 1956-1969

(ALL U.S. FAMILIES)

FAMILY INCOME BEFORE TAXES (in thousands of dollars)
SOURCE: ANNUAL SURVEYS OF CONSUMER FINANCES

OUTSTANDING INSTALLMENT DEBT (1957-1959 dollars)

of $10,000 in 1955 held, on average, $445 of outstanding installment debt when they were interviewed in early 1956. Four years later, families with comparable incomes held an average of $540 in unpaid installment debt balances. Although the 1960 figures are for spending units and the 1965 figures for family units, the upward shift in the debt-to-income function appears to have continued throughout the first half of the decade of the 1960's. Moreover, there is no indication that the upward shifts in the function that occured during the 1950's and early 1960's came to a halt between 1965 and 1969.

From 1965 to 1969 the amount of outstanding installment debt held by families at similar income levels increased very markedly, even after correcting for inflation. Increases were especially large for families with incomes of $8,000 or more.

The upward shift in the installment debt-income function in the late 1960's seems especially significant since it occurred despite a sharp decline in consumer sentiment which began in early 1966 and from which consumers had not fully recovered by late 1969 and despite rising costs of borrowing which persisted throughout the period.

Chapter 3

FOUR-YEAR VERSUS ONE-YEAR RELATIONS

Chapter 2 discussed the relation of expenditures and installment debt balances to income using averages over four consecutive years. Using data averaged over several years is at least one method of handling the problems of errors in independent variables and limited dependent variables which are often encountered in cross-sectional studies where data from only a single year are available. This chapter discusses differences between distributions based upon four-year average data and a single year's data from the panel. It points out some additional advantages of using four years of data rather than data from a single survey only.

For simplicity of exposition, all comparisons are between four-year panel averages and data from the third wave of the panel. The choice of the third year of the panel is arbitrary. Any year of the panel would yield similar results in all important respects.

The Distribution of Expenditures and Debt

In any given year, very many families allocate none or only a very small portion of their total income after federal taxes to investments in major consumer durables. During the calendar year 1968, for example, one-third of the families in the panel made no major purchase at all, and over 20 percent made purchases totaling less than 5 percent of their income for that year (Table 3-1).[1] In contrast, over the entire four years, only 3 percent of the families made no major purchases and fewer than a third of the families allocated as little as 5 percent of their income to expenditures on automobiles and major household durables. At the other extreme, 14 percent of the families in

---

[1]While families with expenditure to income ratios on durables of 25 percent or more are excluded from the analysis in the rest of the book, all families are included here.

the panel made purchases equal to or exceeding 25 percent of their income in 1968, while only about 2 percent spent as much as 25 percent of their income for cars and major household durables over four years.

Despite the great disparity in the distribution of expenditures in one year and over four years, the average expenditure per family in the third year of the panel differs hardly at all from the mean annual expenditure when data over four successive years are considered. The means are shown at the bottom of Table 3-2. On the basis of the standard deviations shown in Table 3-2, using data spanning four years reduces the amount of dispersion of expenditures to about half that observed over the usual arbitrary 12-month accounting period.

The distribution of outstanding installment debt in one year coincides more closely to the distribution of average levels of outstanding installment debt over four years than do single year and four-year average expenditure distributions (Tables 3-3 and 3-4). In contrast to one-year and four-year average expenditures, where the proportion of families having no major expenditure in one year is almost 10 times as great as the proportion of families having no major expenditure over four years, the proportion of families with no outstanding debt in one year (38 percent) is only twice as great as the proportion of families who had no outstanding balances at the time of any of the four successive annual interviews (19 percent). As in the case of expenditures, the average amount of outstanding installment debt at the time of the third interview ($1,025) is virtually identical to the four-year average ($1,003).

The similarity of the one-year and four-year distribution of installment debt balances is not surprising. Expenditures on cars and major household durables are very disjunctive, both because of the high unit prices of most durables and the need to replace individual goods fairly infrequently. Moreover, once a major outlay occurs, the family may need time to accumulate the liquidity necessary for another major purchase. Installment debt, on the other hand, represents an effort on the part of families to even out the impact of major investments in consumer durables on their financial position by extending the payment for such purchases over several periods. One might expect, then, that the one-year distribution of debt would look less different from the four-year average distribution than would the distribution of expenditures.[2]

---

[2]Just how closely the distribution of outstanding installment debt at one point in time approximates a distribution derived from observations at several different points in time depends upon the average term of the debt held by families and how quickly they take on new debts once old obligations are fulfilled. Katona and Mueller examined the factors associated with the incurrence of new debt using data collected at the time of the 1964 tax cut. Of the nine factors studied, having completed the repayment of an installment loan during the period was the second most important predictor of new debt incurrence. George Katona and Eva Mueller, *Consumer Responses to Income Increases,* The Brookings Institution, 1968, pp. 123-131.

Table 3-1

DISTRIBUTION OF ONE-YEAR AND FOUR-YEAR RATIOS
OF DURABLE EXPENDITURES TO INCOME
(Percentage Distribution)

Ratio of Expenditure to Income	One-Year Distribution	Four-Year Distribution
No major expenditure	33	3
Less than 5.0 percent	24	26
5.0-9.9 percent	14	33
10.0-14.9 percent	7	23
15.0-19.9 percent	5	9
20.0-24.9 percent	3	4
25.0-29.9 percent	5	1
30.0-34.9 percent	4	*
35.0-39.9 percent	2	1
40.0 percent or more	3	*
Total	100	100
Mean Ratio	9.2	8.9

*Less than one-half of one percent.

Table 3-2

DISTRIBUTION OF A SINGLE YEAR'S EXPENDITURES ON MAJOR DURABLES
AND FOUR-YEAR AVERAGE ANNUAL EXPENDITURES
(Percentage Distribution)

Annual Expenditures	One-Year Distribution	Four-Year Distribution
None	33	3
$1-249	13	17
$250-499	13	15
$500-749	8	16
$750-999	5	16
$1,000-1,499	5	20
$1,500-1,999	5	8
$2,000-2,499	4	3
$2,500-2,999	5	1
$3,000 or more	9	1
Total	100	100
Mean Expenditure	886	835
One Standard Deviation	1263	655

Table 3-3

DISTRIBUTION OF ONE-YEAR AND FOUR-YEAR RATIOS OF OUTSTANDING
INSTALLMENT DEBT TO INCOME

(Percentage Distribution)

Ratio of Debt to Income	One-Year Distribution	Four-Year Average Distribution
No debt	38	19
Less than 5.0 percent	13	21
5.0-9.9 percent	12	18
10.0-14.9 percent	10	15
15.0-19.9 percent	7	9
20.0-24.9 percent	5	7
25.0-29.9 percent	4	4
30.0-34.9 percent	3	2
35.0-39.9 percent	2	1
40.0 percent or more	6	4
Total	100	100
Mean Ratio	11.0	11.3

Table 3-4

DISTRIBUTION OF ONE-YEAR AND FOUR-YEAR AVERAGE
OUTSTANDING INSTALLMENT DEBT
(Percentage Distribution)

Outstanding Installment Debt	One-Year Distribution	Four-Year Average Distribution
None	38	19
$1-99	3	7
$100-199	4	5
$200-499	9	13
$500-999	12	18
$1,000-1,999	17	23
$2,000-2,999	8	9
$3,000 or more	9	6
Total	100	100
Mean Debt Outstanding	1024	1003
One Standard Deviation	1673	1232

Comparative Relationships with Income

The one-year and four-year relations of expenditures and income differ in two notable respects. As shown in Table 3-5, there is a distinct bulge in the middle of the income distribution for the one-year data, implying, on the basis of one-year data alone, that families with an income between $7,500 and $10,000 spend proportionately more of their income on consumer durables. The middle-income bulge in rates of expenditure on major durables is not peculiar to the panel. For instance, Morgan noted this same pattern in data collected in the early 1950's.[3]

The second respect in which the four-year relation differs from the one-year relation is expected. The degree of heterogeneity of expenditures within income groups is greatly reduced by using a four-year accounting period. As shown by the standard deviations in columns (2) and (4) of Table 3-5, the amount of dispersion of expenditures about the mean of the income group is about twice as great for the one-year data.

All in all, the comparisons in Table 3-5 indicate that one-year data yield estimates of the relation of expenditures to income that are quite similar to those obtained using a longer accounting period, except for families with an income between $7,500 and $10,000. However, data from the panel may overstate the similarity of the relations obtained by using different accounting periods. When data on the same families are available from more than one interview, it is possible to correct certain inconsistencies and resolve ambiguities of reporting that cannot be resolved when only a single interview with the family is available. Moreover, after the fourth and final wave of data collection the entire set of interviews were re-edited in order to check for purchases that were reported as occuring in more than one year. For some purchases, especially of automobiles, double-counting can substantially increase the estimate of expenditures on consumer durables as a proportion of income for a family. Also, editors were able to reconstruct certain major purchases that were never reported but were detected by the appearance of new debt or a car that the family had not previously owned.[4] Since corrections were made to data tapes each year as new inconsistencies and reporting errors were discovered and since tapes with uncorrected data were not preserved, it is not possible to assess how greatly the data for a single year of the panel were improved by the availability of data from previous and forthcoming panel years.

---

[3]James N. Morgan, "Consumer Investment Expenditures," *The American Economic Review,* May, 1958, pp. 874-902.

[4]For a discussion and some estimates of the tendency of respondents, when interviewed in household surveys, to allocate expenditures either to earlier or later time periods than when the expenditures actually occurred, see John Neder and Joseph Waksberg, "A Study of Response Errors in Expenditures Data from Household Surveys," *Journal of the American Statistical Association,* March, 1964, pp. 18-55.

Table 3-5

RATIO OF DURABLE EXPENDITURES TO INCOME IN A SINGLE YEAR AND
OVER FOUR YEARS BY INCOME
(Class Means and Standard Deviations)

One-Year and Four-Year Average Income	One-Year Ratio of Expenditures to Income	One Standard Deviation	Four-Year Ratio of Expenditures to Income	One Standard Deviation
Less than $3,000	6.7	16.2	5.6	5.7
$3,000-4,999	6.9	13.7	6.5	5.9
$5,000-5,999	8.4	14.1	9.1	6.6
$6,000-7,499	7.9	11.9	9.5	5.9
$7,500-8,499	11.6	15.0	9.1	5.6
$8,500-9,999	10.8	13.3	8.9	5.5
$10,000-12,499	9.3	11.5	8.8	5.1
$12,500-14,999	8.5	10.5	8.6	4.3
$15,000-19,999	7.7	8.7	7.4	4.3
$20,000 or more	6.4	7.4	6.7	4.0
All Families	8.8	12.6	8.4	5.5

Table 3-6 suggests that the gains from averaging outstanding installment debt balances over several years are not nearly so great as the gains from averaging expenditures over a fairly long period. The most substantial differences are at the ends of the distribution of income. Families who had an income of less than $3,000 in the third year of the panel had substantially higher installment debt balances relative to their income for that year than did families whose average level of annual income over the four years of the panel was under $3,000. Similarly, at the upper end of the income distribution, families with an income of $15,000 or more in the third year of the panel had higher ratios of debt to income for that year than did families whose income averaged $15,000 or more over four years. In the case of both families with low incomes and families with relatively high incomes, these differences are likely to reflect recent changes in income status or temporary departures of income from normal levels.

The possible distortion in static relations that may result from using an accounting period as short as one year is only one issue that concerns users of survey data. Most often the analyst wants to measure the overall impact of particular variables and to discover which are relatively more important predictors of some dependent variables or types of behavior.

While a great deal of random variation may not greatly bias fitted relations in ordinary least squares models or remove simple correlations based on group means, it will greatly reduce the amount of variance that can be explained and make conventional tests of significance difficult. Thus, relatively important predictors may not appear significant, and judging the relative importance of predictors may become tenuous if not impossible.

A rough idea of the extent of the difficulties which may confront the analyst of household data is indicated by refitting the regressions presented in Chapter 2 using data covering only one year. Regressions (1) and (2) below are of expenditures on major durables (E) as a function of income (Y) and income squared (Y^2). Regression (1) uses four-year average data, while regression (2) uses data from the third year of the panel. Regressions (3) and (4), showing outstanding installment debt (D) as a function of income and using four-year data and data from the third year of the panel, respectively, include only families with an income of less than $10,000.

$$(1)\ E = -37 + .105\ Y - .000001\ Y^2$$
$$\qquad\qquad (20.8)\qquad (11.2) \qquad\qquad\qquad R^2 = .324$$

$$(2)\ E_3 = 31 + .099\ Y_3 - .000001\ Y_3^2$$
$$\qquad\qquad (11.4)\qquad (7.3) \qquad\qquad\qquad R^2 = .094$$

$$(3)\ D = -217 + .148\ Y$$
$$\qquad\qquad\qquad (13.5) \qquad\qquad\qquad R^2 = .172$$

$$(4) \ D_3 = -144 + .132 \ Y_3$$
$$(10.5) \qquad\qquad\qquad\qquad R^2 = .112$$

Both for expenditures and for outstanding installment debt the fitted relations are virtually identical regardless of whether a four-year or a one-year accounting period is used. The slight downward bias is expected in the estimated slope coefficients on income when a single year's data are used.

The major difference which arises when the shorter accounting period is used is in the proportion of variance explained. In both instances the R^2 is lower for the regression which uses data from the third year of the panel. The difference is especially striking for expenditures on major durables. While income over four years explains fully 32 percent of the variance in expenditures over the same period, income in a single year explains less than 10 percent of the variance in a single year's expenditures on major durables. The impact of the reduction in explained variance using the shorter accounting period is evident in the t-ratios, which appear in parentheses below the slope coefficients, as well. Since income is clearly the dominant determinant of investments in durable goods, the great reduction in its significance as a predictor of one-year expenditures should make it clear how difficult it may be to determine whether other less important determinants are, in fact, important at all when data from only one year are available.

As expected, the reduction in the ability of income to predict outstanding installment debt balances when data from only the third year of the panel is used is less extreme than the reduction for expenditures. The difference is great enough, however, that data on installment debt at a single point in time may somewhat hamper efforts to sort out the various predictors of debt use and their relative importance.

Although we have taken only a very cursory look in this chapter at the effects of aggregating over time, it does seem clear that accounting periods of more than 12 months are both appropriate and advantageous in estimating cross-sectional relations between financial variables. Many factors, of course, enter into the decision of how long an accounting period is best for a particular purpose. However, some notion of the gains of temporal aggregation for the types of relations considered in Chapter 2 is given by tracing the paths of the correlation coefficients as data are aggregated over more years.

The correlation between expenditures and income in the fourth year of the panel was .30. When two years are considered (the third and fourth years) the correlation increases to .38 or by 8 percentage points; when three years are considered, the correlation increases by 7 percentage points to .45; and when all four years are added together, the correlation increases to .47 or by only 2 percentage points. If this trend is at all stable, adding a fifth year would do little, if anything, to reduce further the heterogeneity of expenditures within

Table 3-6

ONE-YEAR AND FOUR-YEAR RATIOS OF OUTSTANDING INSTALLMENT DEBT
TO INCOME BY INCOME
(Class Means and Standard Deviations)

One-Year and Four-Year Average Income	One-Year Ratio of Debt to Income	One Standard Deviation	Four-Year Ratio of Debt to Income	One Standard Deviation
Less than $3,000	7.5	18.1	4.3	6.8
$3,000-4,999	7.3	11.6	8.1	9.7
$5,000-5,999	10.9	15.2	12.0	11.1
$6,000-7,499	11.4	15.4	11.6	11.1
$7,500-8,499	11.4	13.6	11.9	10.4
$8,500-9,999	12.9	13.7	12.3	10.1
$10,000-12,499	10.9	13.0	10.9	10.7
$12,500-14,999	8.9	14.2	9.2	9.7
$15,000-19,999	8.0	12.1	6.8	7.3
$20,000 or more	4.0	8.5	3.2	4.4
All Families	10.0	13.9	10.0	10.2

income groups.[5]

For the relation of debt, a stock which can be adjusted fairly continuously as opposed to expenditures on major durables which cannot, the gains of additional years of data collection are relatively small. The correlation between income and outstanding installment debt in the fourth year of the panel was .16; for the last two years of the panel combined it was .19; and for all four years it was .22. Thus, in estimating static relations with outstanding installment debt, the gain by adding observations at annual intervals beyond two observations may be small.

---

[5]Of course, there is a limit to how long a period one would want to aggregate across. Over very long periods changes in the status of families would become so great that further temporal aggregation would become meaningless and a whole new set of problems would be introduced.

Chapter 4

DEMOGRAPHIC CORRELATES OF INCOME, EXPENDITURES, AND DEBT

In Chapter 2 we examined the relation between expenditures on consumer durables to income and the relation of installment debt to income, using averages over several years, and we made some preliminary comments on the possible implications of these relationships for the expected rate of growth of expenditures on major durables and of outstanding consumer installment credit over the next few years. As pointed out there, any assertions about future changes are based on the assumption that the relationships observed with income reflect only the impact of income. It is possible, however, that the relations that we observe in Chapter 2 do not entirely reflect the longer-run relation of expenditures and installment debt to income, but instead reflect the relation of other variables which are correlated with income.

In this chapter essentially two variables are studied—family life cycle and housing status. It is particularly likely to be true that the demographic composition of the families at the two extremes of the income distribution are different from the demographic composition of the population in general. Thus, the decline in expenditures that we observe at very high incomes and the rapid increase in the proportion of the income allocated to expenditures on major durables as we move from the low income to the middle income range of the income distribution may, in fact, be artificial effects which do not really reflect changes due to income, but rather reflect differences in demographic composition of the families in lower, middle and higher income groups. Similarly, for installment debt some unknown portion of the decline in debt use at high incomes may reflect characteristics other than income itself.

Income and Demographic Characteristics

Table 4-1 shows detailed distributions of the composition of families within income groups for the panel. Seven family characteristics appear in

43

Table 4-1. Six are related to age and family composition, and the seventh is housing status. In order to increase the reliability of the estimates, only four income groups are shown rather than the ten groups distinguished in Chapter 2. However, the income ranges were selected so that differences between them would coincide with the major changes in the slopes of the relations of expenditures and installment debt balances to income described earlier.

As expected, the composition of families in both the lowest and highest income groups differs markedly from the composition of the middle income groups. The less than $5,000 income group contains proportionately more families whose heads were 50 years old or older at the time of the first interview than does any higher income group. There is a striking difference in the proportion of single people in the low income groups. While 10 percent or fewer of the families with average annual incomes of $5,000 or more a year were single, 42 percent of those family units with incomes under $5,000 had single persons as their heads. As shown by the distribution of heads by stage in the family life cycle, the single people in the low income group are almost all either older (over 45) or are single parents with children still living at home. Young single people, although they make up a larger portion of the under $5,000 income group than the $15,000 or more income group, are not especially predominant in the low income group.

Since the panel excluded families whose heads were over age 59 at the time of the first interview, only 6 percent of family heads were retired at the time of the first interview, and an additional 2 percent retired sometime after the first interview took place. Of families with incomes of less than $5,000 a year, however, 21 percent were retired when interviewed for the first time and 8 percent retired sometime in the next three years. Retirees made up 7 percent or less of the families in the other income groups.

The highest income group ($15,000 or more) is dominated by families with middle-aged heads and contains an especially large proportion of families with heads between the ages of 45 and 49. Families with younger heads, on the other hand, make up only a very small proportion of the families in the highest income groups. Almost half of the families who had an average income of $15,000 or more over the four years of the panel had been married for 20 years or more at the time of the initial encounter.

Middle income families in the panel—families with an income between $5,000 and $10,000 a year—are younger than are the families in the two more extreme income groups. Forty-one percent of the families with an income of $5,000 to $9,999 were under age 35 when first interviewed and 42 percent of those with an income of $10,000 to $14,999 were under 40. Young couples, especially with young children, make up a larger proportion of middle income families and are especially obvious in the lower-middle income group. Families who were married less than five years made up twice as large a proportion (17 percent) of families with an average income between $5,000 and

$10,000 than they did of any other income group.

The last family characteristic considered in Table 4-1 is housing status. In any single survey, housing status is clearly defined at the time of the interview. However, over four years many families adjust their housing and change from renters to homeowners once or even more often. Some decision must be made on who is to be labelled a homeowner and who is a renter. Based largely on data from a recent study of movers, the following definitions were used in developing a housing status variable.[1] Families who were homeowners in both the first and last years of the panel were classified as homeowners all four years regardless of any intermediary housing status. Similarly, families who were renting both at the time of the first and the last interview were classified as renters all four years. Families who were renting in the first year of the panel but owned in the last year were classified as having changed status from renter to owner and vice versa for families who owned in the first year.

Obviously some families are misclassified by using these definitions, and misclassifications may be particularly common among those classified as having changed status. However, the margin of error is less than if housing status at the time of a single interview had been accepted as the best measure.

It is well known that most American families prefer to own their own homes and that housing status is closely associated with income. This is no less true of the families in the panel than of other families. Renters make up 42 percent of the low income group and are about twice as frequent among families with an income less than $5,000 than among families with an income between $5,000 and $10,000. The vast majority—over 90 percent—of families with an income of $10,000 or more owned their own home at the beginning of the panel or acquired a home sometime during the first and last interview.

If, as is often asserted, families who rent spend significantly less of their income on durables than do families who own their homes, a substantial part of the difference in the proportion of income invested in cars and major household durables between lower and middle income families, and the differences in installment debt use as well, could be accounted for by differences in housing status rather than by differences in income.

Although families with heads aged 60 or older in early 1967 and unrelated secondary family units were intentionally excluded from the panel, substantial differences in the composition of families at different income levels remain. The general impression from Table 4-1 is that upper income families are older, more established families who own their own homes and are in or near their peak earning years, while middle income families are generally

---

[1]Lansing et al. found that about 13 percent of moves involve the use of temporary quarters and that the length of stay in these quarters varies widely. John B. Lansing, Charles Wade Clifton, and James N. Morgan, *New Homes and Poor People: A Study of Chains of Moves*, The Institute for Social Research, Ann Arbor, Michigan, 1969; especially Appendix C.

younger, less established, often recently married, and may have some time to go before they near their peak earnings. Low income families include substantial numbers of single people who, though young to retire, are not in the labor force. About half of the single people in the low income group are separated, divorced or widowed parents with children still living at home.

Not only are there differences in the demographic composition of families at different income levels, but the differences are such that we might expect them to lead to differences in installment debt use and in investments in major consumer durables, quite aside from any differences that could be attributed to the differences in income itself. The concentration at lower incomes of renters and single people may account for more modest demand for durables and use of installment debt among lower income families. In contrast, the greater concentration of younger families with an income from $5,000 to $9,999 may account for a substantial amount of the heavy debt use and high expenditure rates on durables in that income group.

Much of this is conjecture, of course, but it is the sort of conjecture that is encountered often in household studies of the demand for consumer durables. Moreover, much of this speculation can be at least provisionally confirmed or tentatively rejected on the basis of simple but more detailed analysis.

Life Cycle and Expenditures

To test for differences in expenditure behavior among income and life cycle groups, average ratios of expenditures on major durables to income were calculated for each of the cells in Table 4-1 and are shown in Table 4-2. Some of the categories shown in Table 4-1 have been collapsed in Table 4-2 in order to obtain somewhat more stable estimates of the means. However, collapsing categories was done only after careful examination of the full distributions in order not to remove variations which might be significant in explaining the observed differences in expenditure rates between income groups or the differences between family composition and life cycle groups. The reader must be warned that many of the cells are very small. However, on the grounds that having some observations reduces the error from infinity to some finite number, the means for all cells are shown. The number of families in each cell is shown in parentheses below the mean.

The ultimate impact of the distribution of families by family composition and by life cycle characteristics among income groups on the expenditure and installment debt functions shown in Chapter 2 depends upon two things: (1) the extent to which families who have the same income but who differ in other ways differ also in their behavior; and (2) the extent to which families who differ with respect to income but who are similar in other ways spend differing proportions of their income on major durables. Table 4-2 must be viewed from both perspectives. Differences between expenditure rates down the columns of Table 4-2 reflect differences among families owing to demographic characteristics. Differences in expenditure rates across the rows of Table 4-2 reflect differences that are due mainly to income. Hence, by comparing rows and columns we can get some notion of the extent to which differences in expenditure rates are the result of differences in income level, and to what extent they do not reflect differences in income but rather differences in the demographic composition of the various income groups.

A perusal of the columns of Table 4-2 is convincing evidence that families in different stages of the family life cycle, and differently composed, differ in the proportion of their income they spend on major consumer durables. The differences in expenditure rates between single people and married couples are especially striking. Single people spend 2 to 3 percent less of their income on major consumer durables than do married couples regardless of income level.

Although one of the striking differences between the low income group and other income groups is in the age of family heads, Table 4-2 indicates that age alone probably contributes little to differences in expenditure rates among income groups. For all families taken together, expenditure rates fall consistently with age. Once income is controlled for, however, expenditure rates of older and younger families differ hardly at all. Thus, much of the apparent effect of age reflects differences in income.

Regardless of income, families in the younger life cycle groups tend to spend a larger fraction of their income on durables than do older people. The substantially lower proportion of income spent by older married couples in the low income group whose children have all left home, may be in part the result of the number of these families with retired heads. However, even among high income families, where few heads are retired, families whose children have left home have lower than average expenditure rates.

While the fact that there are important differences in expenditure patterns between demographic groups is substantiated by Table 4-2, scanning the rows of the table also shows that differences between income groups persist even for families who are in the same stage of their life cycle. For example, although young couples who were childless at the time of the first interview spent larger fractions of their incomes on durables than older more established families with similar incomes, it is still true that young childless couples with an average of less than $5,000 a year or more than $15,000 a year invested proportionately less in durables than did young childless couples with an income between $5,000 and $15,000. Similarly, among single people, those with an income of less than $5,000 or more than $15,000 spent proportionately less of their income on durables than did single people in the middle income groups.

On the basis of Table 4-2, two conclusions seem warranted. First, because of the high concentration of single people, older families, and retired family heads in the under $5,000 income group, and because of the concentration of younger, more recently married families in the middle income groups, the differences in expenditure rates between the lower and middle income groups shown in Chapter 2 are likely to reflect differences in family composition as well as differences due purely to income. For high income families, the case is less clear. On the one hand, the high income group contains a disproportionately small percentage of young families. The lack of such families would tend to lower average expenditure rates at high incomes. On the other hand, among high income families there are also fewer older families with retired heads and almost no single people. Both of these groups would tend to pull down average expenditure rates at high incomes. The second conclusion that is warranted is that differences in expenditure rates among income groups would remain even if there were no differences in family composition and life cycle among income groups.

Table 4-2 does show that the lower rates of expenditures on durables of high income and low income families are not simply or largely the result of differences in family composition or other life cycle characteristics. However, the table does not provide a very concise estimate of the extent to which the nonproportional relation of expenditures on durables to income might be reduced if families in differing demographic situations were more evenly distributed throughout the entire range of income. There are a number of methods that could be used to obtain such an estimate. One of the most straightforward would be to reweight families at different income levels so that the distribution of families by family life cycle would be similar at each income level. Then, the expenditure-income function could be recalculated based on these weights.[2] There is yet another method which, though less precise, is also less painstaking. The evidence presented in Table 4-2 suggests that family life cycle and income, although correlated, do not interact to any great extent. If the joint impact of being in a particular life cycle-income group does not have a larger impact on expenditures than would be expected by simply adding the independent impacts of the two variables together, then regression analysis can be used to approximate how the relation of income and expenditures might be changed if the composition of families by family life cycle were more nearly equal at all income levels.[3]

[2]This method was actually used by Lansing and Lyndall in studying differences in saving rates between the United States and the United Kingdom in the 1950's. Reweighting the U.S. survey data to conform to the British distributions on several demographic characteristics reduced the differential in saving rates between the countries. John B. Lansing and Harold Lyndall, "An Anglo-American Comparison of Personal Savings," *Bulletin*, August, 1960, pp. 225-258.

[3]The cells in Table 4-2 are too small and the estimates too unstable to reveal any but the strongest interactions between income and family life cycle. However, the general impression is that income and family life cycle do not interact to any great extent in determining the proportion of their income that families allocate to investments in major consumer durables.

Table 4-1

DEMOGRAPHIC COMPOSITION OF AVERAGE ANNUAL INCOME GROUPS

(Percentage Distribution)

Demographic Characteristic[1]	All Families	Average Annual Income			
		Less than $5,000	$5,000- 9,999	$10,000- 14,999	$15,000 or more
Age of Head					
Under 25	7	7	11	2	*
25-29	12	8	16	9	5
30-34	13	11	14	13	9
35-39	13	7	12	18	15
40-44	13	10	12	16	16
45-49	15	13	12	17	26
50-54	14	21	12	15	15
55-59	13	23	11	10	14
Total	100	100	100	100	100
Marital Status					
Married all years	79	45	80	91	89
Single all years	12	42	10	5	2
Single to married	3	4	5	2	1
Other, more than one change	6	9	5	2	8
Total	100	100	100	100	100
Life Cycle Stage in Family[2]					
Young, single	4	5	5	3	1
Young, married, no children	6	3	7	6	4
Young, married, youngest child under 6	29	16	35	28	23
Young, married, youngest child 6 or older	15	4	15	19	17
Older, married, children at home	19	15	16	22	32
Older, married, no children at home	15	16	12	18	21
Older, single	6	21	5	1	2
Any age, single with children	6	20	5	3	*
Total	100	100	100	100	100

Table 4-1 (con't)

Demographic Characteristic	All Families	Average Annual Income			
		Less than $5,000	$5,000- 9,999	$10,000- 14,999	$15,000 or more
Years Married					
Single	16	45	15	7	4
Married					
2 or fewer	3	3	9	3	1
3-4	4	5	8	4	3
5-9	13	6	17	16	15
10-19	27	12	27	33	28
20 or more	37	27	24	37	49
Total	100	100	100	100	100
Retirement Status					
Retired in 1967	6	21	5	1	2
Retired in 1970	2	8	2	2	1
Not retired	92	71	93	97	97
Total	100	100	100	100	100
Presence and Number of Children					
Single:					
No children	10	26	10	4	3
Children	6	20	5	3	1
Married:					
No children	21	19	19	25	24
One child	18	11	20	18	16
Two children	20	11	20	22	28
Three children	13	6	12	16	18
Four or more	12	7	14	12	10
Total	100	100	100	100	100

Table 4-1 (con't)

Demographic Characteristic	All Families	Average Annual Income			
		Less than $5,000	$5,000–9,999	$10,000–14,999	$15,000 or more
Housing Status					
Owner	66	35	62	81	89
Renter	20	42	23	10	3
Renting to owning	9	11	10	7	4
Owning to renting	2	2	3	1	3
Other	3	10	2	1	1
Total	100	100	100	100	100

---

*Less than one-half of one percent.

[1]Age, family life cycle, years married and presence and number of children are as of the time of the first interview with the family. Marital, retirement and housing status take into account changes in status over the course of the panel as well as the initial status of the family.

[2]Families with heads under age 45 are classified as young. Older families are those whose head was age 45 or older at the time of the first interview.

Table 4-2

MEAN FOUR-YEAR RATIO OF EXPENDITURES ON DURABLES TO INCOME
WITHIN INCOME AND LIFE CYCLE CHARACTERISTICS

(Cell Means and Frequencies)[1]

Demographic Characteristic[2]	All Families	Average Annual Income			
		Less than $5,000	$5,000- 9,999	$10,000- 14,999	$15,000 or more
Age of Head					
Under 30	9.7 (266)	5.8 (28)	10.7 (187)	8.8 (43)	8.5 (8)
30-39	8.4 (371)	6.2 (36)	9.3 (180)	8.2 (119)	6.8 (36)
40-49	8.1 (392)	6.7 (44)	7.8 (161)	9.6 (124)	7.3 (63)
50 or older	7.8 (377)	5.9 (83)	8.7 (154)	8.3 (97)	6.8 (43)
Marital Status					
Married all years	8.8 (1111)	7.4 (86)	9.3 (542)	8.9 (349)	7.3 (134)
Single all years	6.0 (172)	4.9 (79)	7.4 (71)	6.5 (19)	1.4 (3)
Single to married	10.1 (48)	7.7 (8)	10.7 (31)	10.7 (8)	– (1)
Other, more than one change	7.6 (75)	4.8 (18)	9.5 (38)	7.3 (7)	6.3 (12)
Stage in Family Life Cycle					
Young, single	8.4 (58)	6.9 (9)	9.4 (37)	7.0 (11)	– (1)
Young, married, no children	10.2 (84)	7.3 (6)	11.4 (48)	9.1 (24)	8.4 (6)
Young, married, youngest child under 6	8.7 (412)	6.8 (31)	9.4 (240)	8.3 (106)	7.4 (35)
Young, married, youngest child 6 or older	9.1 (208)	6.5 (8)	9.8 (103)	8.9 (72)	7.3 (25)
Older, married, children at home	8.5 (266)	8.6 (28)	8.2 (106)	9.6 (84)	7.5 (48)
Older, married, no children at home	8.0 (212)	5.7 (30)	8.9 (81)	8.6 (70)	6.5 (31)
Older, single	6.0 (82)	5.2 (40)	7.1 (34)	6.9 (5)	2.0 (3)
Any age, single with children	6.7 (84)	4.6 (39)	8.6 (33)	8.9 (11)	– (1)

Table 4-2 (con't)

Demographic Characteristic	All Families	Average Annual Income			
		Less than $5,000	$5,000- 9,999	$10,000- 14,999	$15,000 or more
Years Married[4]					
2 or fewer	10.1 (80)	5.3 (5)	10.8 (60)	9.2 (13)	7.1 (2)
3-4	9.4 (86)	7.5 (10)	10.2 (55)	8.9 (16)	6.4 (5)
5-9	9.0 (211)	8.0 (12)	9.8 (116)	8.5 (61)	6.9 (22)
10-19	8.2 (369)	7.0 (23)	8.5 (181)	8.7 (124)	6.7 (41)
20 or more	8.6 (433)	6.6 (51)	9.1 (166)	9.1 (142)	7.8 (74)
Retirement Status					
Retired in 1966	6.0 (82)	5.2 (40)	7.1 (34)	6.9 (5)	2.0 (3)
Retired in 1970	7.1 (36)	4.4 (15)	10.0 (13)	7.3 (7)	– (1)
Not retired	8.6 (1288)	6.6 (136)	9.3 (635)	8.8 (371)	7.2 (146)
Number of Children[3]					
None	8.6 (295)	5.9 (36)	9.8 (129)	8.7 (94)	6.9 (36)
One	9.4 (252)	10.3 (21)	9.4 (139)	9.4 (68)	8.7 (24)
Two	8.8 (285)	6.8 (22)	9.7 (135)	8.9 (86)	7.1 (42)
Three	8.9 (181)	6.8 (11)	9.6 (82)	9.1 (60)	6.6 (28)
Four or more	7.6 (169)	4.9 (13)	7.8 (93)	7.7 (48)	7.8 (15)
All Families	8.4 (1406)	6.1 (191)	9.2 (682)	8.7 (383)	7.1 (149)

---

[1]Numbers in parentheses are cell frequencies. Ratios are in percent.

[2]Age, family life cycle, years married and number of children are the status of the family at the time of the first interview.

[3]See Footnote Table 4-1 for definitions of categories.

[4]People who were single in the first year of the panel are excluded.

Since the effects of sociological characteristics are seldom linear and often defy concise, simple, mathematical formulation, dummy variables were employed in the analysis. The particular technique used here differs somewhat from the dummy variable techniques most often used. First, the sample is divided into any number of desired categories on each of the predictors to be included in the analysis. For any one characteristic, such as family life cycle, the categories must be both all-inclusive and mutually exclusive. The regression is then estimated under the constraint that the constant term be equal to the mean of the dependent variable. The coefficient on each subgroup (category of a predictor) then becomes the deviation of the mean of that subgroup from the mean of the dependent variable, after adjusting for any abnormality of the distribution of families in the subgroup within the subgroups or categories of other variables included in the regression.[4]

The results of the regression analysis are shown in Table 4-3. In addition to average annual income and family life cycle at the time of the first interview, a variable which accounts for major changes in life cycle is also included. Since, as shown by Table 4-2, changes in life cycle stage may substantially effect expenditure rates on major durables, such changes must be taken into account in analyzing expenditures over a period as long as three years.

For all families in the panel, the mean proportion of income allocated to purchases of major consumer durables over the entire four years was 8.4 percent. Two sets of deviations from this mean are shown in Table 4-3. The first are deviations of the means of the income subgroups shown from the sample mean of 8.4 before any adjustment was made for differences in family life cycle. Adding these unadjusted deviations to the sample mean of 8.4 yields the average expenditure to income ratio (in percent) of the income subgroup, and the resulting subgroup means will be the same as those shown in Column (3) of Table 2-1. The second set of deviations, the adjusted deviations, are the estimated regression coefficients simultaneously adjusted for the composition of the subgroup defined by other predictors in the regression. Since the coefficients were derived by adjusting the means of subgroups, the stability of the estimates depends upon the number of families who fall into each of the cells in the analysis. Thus, the number of families in each subgroup is also shown in Table 4-3.

As expected, not taking account simultaneously of the disproportionate number of families at lower income levels who are either older or single does reduce expenditure rates at lower income levels, and hence exaggerates the responsiveness of expenditures to differences in income between the lower end and the middle of the income distribution. For families with an income of less than $3,000 over the four years, for example, the unadjusted devia-

---

[4]For a complete explanation of this regression technique see Frank Andrews, James N. Morgan, and John Sonquist, *Multiple Classification Analysis,* The Institute for Social Research, Ann Arbor, Michigan, 1967.

Table 4-3

PROPORTION OF INCOME SPENT ON MAJOR DURABLES BEFORE AND AFTER ADJUSTMENT
FOR DIFFERENCES IN DEMOGRAPHIC SITUATION

Predictors	Number of Families	Unadjusted Deviations	Adjusted Deviations
Average Annual Income ($B^2=.029$)			
Under $3,000	81	-2.9	-1.9
$3,000-4,999	110	-1.9	-1.2
$5,000-5,999	110	.7	.7
$6,000-7,499	195	1.1	1.2
$7,500-8,499	166	.7	.6
$8,500-9,999	211	.5	.3
$10,000-12,499	250	.4	.2
$12,500-14,999	133	.2	-.1
$15,000-19,999	87	-1.0	-1.2
$20,000 or more	63	-1.7	-1.9
Stage in Family Life Cycle ($B^2=.027$)			
Young, single	58	0.0	-1.3
Young, married, no children	84	1.8	1.6
Young, married, youngest child under 6	412	.3	.3
Young, married, youngest child 6 or older	208	.6	.6
Older, married, children at home	266	.1	.2
Older, married, no children at home	212	-.5	.1
Older, single	82	-2.4	-2.0
Any age, single, with children	84	-1.7	-2.0
Major Change in Life Cycle ($B^2=.017$)			
Got married	48	1.6	3.2
Became single	54	-1.5	-1.6
Last child left home	71	.8	.7
No children to having children	44	2.1	.2
More than one change in marital status	21	1.1	1.5
No major change	1168	-.1	-.1

NOTE: The dependent variable is the percent of four-year income spent on major durables. The mean of the dependent variable = 8.4 (constant term); the R^2 for the regression was .057. Unadjusted deviations are univariate subgroup means expressed as deviations from the sample mean of 8.4. The adjusted deviations are dummy variable regression co-efficients under the constraint that the weighted sum of the set of coefficients for a predictor equals zero. This yields the sample mean of the dependent variable as the constant term of the regression. There were 1406 families in the regression analysis.

tion in expenditure rates is -2.9 percentage points. However, once differences in family life cycle are adjusted for, the deviation is reduced to -1.9 percentage points. Similarly, for families with an income between $3,000 and $5,000, taking account of family life cycle reduces the amount by which these families' expenditure rates deviate from those of families with incomes above $5,000. The implication of these data is that any substantial increase or redistribution of income to families who are currently among the poorest in the United States would result in less growth in the demand for consumer durables than predicted on a basis of the cross-section relation of expenditures to income alone.

Of more concern for projecting the future growth of the demand for major consumer durables than what happens at the lower end of the income distribution is whether there are any substantial adjustments in expenditure rates at relatively high income levels. The data in Table 4-3 undermine the hypothesis that the lower expenditure rates on major durables observed at higher income levels in cross-section data are the result of shifts in preferences over the family life cycle and the correlation between family life cycle and income. To the contrary, taking account of family life cycle leads to a more rapid decline in the demand for durables at income levels of $10,000 a year or more (in 1966-1969 dollars).

This analysis tends to confirm the assertion made in Chapter 2 that we might expect continued increases in real income to exert a downward pressure on the rate of growth of the demand for consumer durables like automobiles and major household appliances, and perhaps even expect a decline in the proportion of aggregate income allocated to expenditures on conventional durables in the not-too-distant future.[5]

Life Cycle and Installment Debt Balances

An analysis similar to the tabular analysis for expenditure rates is repeated for installment debt in Table 4-4. The findings from the table of installment debt to income ratios within income and family life cycle groups follow in broad outline those for expenditures. People who were single all four years maintained lower ratios of installment debt to income than married couples; those who were most recently married generally maintained higher installment debt balances than other families; and families with retired heads maintained lower balances than did families whose heads were still actively participating in the labor force. Among life cycle groups, younger families, especially those with no children or young children, generally maintained

---

[5]A number of other regression analyses were run which included age and retirement status as well as family life cycle, changes in family life cycle, and income. Including these other variables in the regressions did not change the estimates of the adjusted deviations from mean expenditures for the various income groups.

Table 4-4

MEAN RATIOS OF INSTALLMENT DEBT TO INCOME
WITHIN INCOME AND LIFE CYCLE CHARACTERISTICS
(Cell Means and Frequencies)[1]

Demographic Characteristic[2]	All Families	Average Annual Income			
		Less than $5,000	$5,000– 9,999	$10,000– 14,999	$15,000 or more
Age of Head					
Under 25	15.8 (97)	11.9 (19)	16.0 (71)	23.3 (7)	12.8 (8)
25–29	12.0 (175)	5.9 (16)	13.6 (114)	9.7 (37)	4.8 (14)
30–34	12.6 (178)	7.5 (22)	13.9 (91)	14.5 (51)	4.2 (22)
35–39	10.2 (190)	6.7 (14)	13.2 (85)	9.2 (69)	4.3 (24)
40–44	9.1 (184)	4.5 (19)	10.8 (82)	10.0 (59)	6.8 (38)
45–49	9.3 (209)	8.2 (25)	10.0 (81)	10.3 (65)	4.8 (22)
50–54	8.6 (198)	3.9 (39)	11.7 (79)	9.6 (58)	2.8 (21)
55–59	6.1 (178)	6.1 (43)	6.6 (74)	6.7 (40)	– (0)
Marital Status					
Married all years	10.3 (1104)	7.0 (87)	12.0 (532)	10.3 (352)	5.7 (133)
Single all years	6.9 (173)	4.7 (79)	9.2 (72)	8.4 (19)	0.0 (3)
Single to married	14.3 (54)	12.7 (11)	15.5 (34)	11.7 (8)	– (1)
Other, more than one change	10.5 (78)	7.8 (20)	13.8 (39)	10.0 (7)	2.2 (12)
Stage in Family Life Cycle[3]					
Young, single	10.2 (63)	6.1 (11)	12.2 (40)	8.2 (11)	– (1)
Young, married, no children	12.1 (85)	5.2 (6)	14.0 (48)	11.7 (25)	5.6 (6)
Young, married, youngest child under 6	11.9 (409)	9.0 (35)	13.5 (232)	11.5 (107)	5.8 (35)
Young, married youngest child 6 or older	11.5 (207)	8.0 (8)	13.7 (102)	10.9 (72)	4.8 (25)
Older, married, children at home	9.1 (267)	7.5 (26)	10.1 (108)	9.7 (85)	6.4 (48)
Older, married, no children at home	7.0 (210)	5.3 (31)	7.5 (79)	8.6 (70)	3.8 (30)
Older, single	6.1 (84)	5.6 (42)	7.2 (34)	5.9 (5)	4.7 (3)
Any age, single with children	9.8 (84)	5.5 (38)	13.9 (34)	12.1 (11)	– (1)

Table 4-4 (con't)

Demographic Characteristic	All Families	Less than $5,000	$5,000-9,999	$10,000-14,999	$15,000 or more
Years Married					
2 or fewer	13.6 (83)	9.2 (6)	13.6 (61)	16.4 (14)	4.9 (2)
3-4	12.7 (88)	10.5 (13)	14.2 (54)	11.8 (16)	4.9 (5)
5-9	12.0 (206)	7.9 (12)	13.5 (110)	12.0 (62)	6.5 (22)
10-19	10.2 (366)	6.7 (23)	12.5 (178)	8.6 (124)	4.5 (41)
20 or more	8.6 (432)	6.3 (50)	9.5 (166)	9.7 (143)	5.7 (73)
Retirement Status					
Retired in 1966	6.1 (84)	5.6 (42)	7.2 (34)	5.8 (5)	0.5 (3)
Retired in 1970	5.9 (34)	4.1 (14)	6.4 (12)	9.5 (7)	- (1)
Not retired	10.4 (1291)	7.0 (141)	12.3 (631)	10.4 (374)	5.4 (145)
Number of Children					
None	8.5 (294)	5.3 (37)	10.0 (127)	9.4 (95)	3.9 (35)
One	11.4 (253)	12.0 (22)	12.8 (138)	9.8 (69)	7.3 (24)
Two	10.2 (286)	6.9 (23)	12.2 (135)	10.5 (86)	5.5 (42)
Three	11.6 (178)	7.1 (11)	13.0 (78)	13.8 (61)	4.6 (28)
Four or more	10.8 (167)	5.6 (13)	13.1 (91)	8.7 (48)	7.3 (15)
All Families	10.0 (1409)	6.5 (197)	12.0 (677)	10.3 (386)	5.3 (148)

[1] Numbers in parentheses are cell frequencies. Ratios are in percent.

[2] Age, family life cycle, years married and number of children are the status of the family at the time of the first interview.

[3] See footnote to Table 4-1 for definitions of categories.

[4] People who were single in the first year of the panel are excluded.

larger installment debt balances than older families whose children had left home before the time of the first interview.

While the findings for installment debt are similar to those for expenditures, there are a few noteworthy differences. In the case of expenditures, differences in family composition, the age of the family head, and the like, lead to differences in expenditure rates of only one or two percentage points for families at similar income levels. Among these same groups, however, differences in the ratio of installment debt to average annual income of four percentage points or more are common.

There is another notable distinction between the effects of family characteristics on consumer durable expenditures and installment debt balances: among families with an income of $15,000 or more, life cycle characteristics seem to have less systematic impact on the extensiveness of installment debt commitments than upon expenditures on durables. Only for the very young families—of which there are very few in the over $15,000 income group—do installment debt balances relative to income seem to differ very much from the balances held by high income families in other stages of the family life cycle. The lack of any significant relationship here suggests, even before running a multivariate analysis, that holding differences in family life cycle constant should have little impact on the relation of installment debt use and income at the upper-end of the income distribution.

The estimated impact of income on the use of installment debt before and after adjustment for differences in family composition is presented in Table 4-5. As discussed in Chapter 2 and shown by the unadjusted deviations in the installment debt to income ratios (in percent) in Table 4-5, low income families maintain installment debt balances which are only about one-half as great, relative to their incomes, as the balances maintained by middle income families. As income rises above $5,000 per year, average installment debt balances tend to grow at almost exactly the same rate as income, up to income levels of around $10,000. Thereafter, the deviations from the mean fall at successively higher incomes and at incomes of $20,000 or more outstanding installment debt balances constitute on the average hardly more than 3 percent of annual family income.

Adjusting for differences in demographic situation does little to alter the basic relation between income and average outstanding installment debt balances. At low incomes the adjusted deviations are smaller than the unadjusted ones. However, the adjustment does not nearly equalize the debt to income ratios between lower and middle income families. Thus, even after taking account of the disproportionate number of older and single people at lower income levels, it remains true that families with low incomes generally do not maintain outstanding installment debt balances that are nearly so high, relative to their incomes, as the balances maintained by middle income families.

Including family life cycle in the regression analysis does reduce the aver-

Table 4-5

RATIO OF OUTSTANDING INSTALLMENT DEBT TO INCOME BEFORE AND AFTER ADJUSTMENT
FOR DIFFERENCES IN INCOME AND DEMOGRAPHIC SITUATION

Predictors	Number of Families	Unadjusted Deviations	Adjusted Deviations
Average Annual Income (B^2=.052)			
Under $3,000	83	−5.7	−4.7
$3,000-4,999	114	−1.9	−1.2
$5,000-5,999	111	1.9	2.0
$6,000-7,499	194	1.5	1.4
$7,500-8,499	165	1.9	1.5
$8,5000-9,999	207	2.3	1.8
$10,000-12,499	253	.9	.8
$12,500-14,999	133	−.9	−.8
$15,000-19,999	86	−3.2	−3.2
$20,000 or more	63	−6.8	−6.5
Stage in Family Life Cycle (B^2=.030)			
Young, single	63	.1	−2.4
Young, married, no children	85	2.1	2.2
Young, married, youngest child under 6	409	1.9	1.7
Young, married, youngest child 6 or older	207	1.4	1.3
Older, married, children at home	267	−1.0	−.7
Older, married, no children at home	210	−3.0	−2.4
Older, single	84	−3.9	−2.9
Any age, single, with children	84	−.2	−1.0
Major Changes in Life Cycle (B^2=.013)			
Got married	54	4.2	5.6
Became single	57	.5	.5
Last child left home	70	.1	1.0
No children to having children	44	2.2	−.7
More than one change in marital status	21	.5	1.4
No major change	1163	−.3	−.3

NOTE: The mean of the dependent variable = 10.0 (constant term); the R^2 for
the regression is .091. The dependent variable is the ratio (in percent) of outstanding installment debt to four-year income. Unadjusted
deviations are univariate subgroup means expressed as deviations from
the sample mean of 10.0. The adjusted deviations are dummy variable
regression coefficients under the constraint that the weighted sum of
the set of coefficients for a predictor equals zero. This yields the
sample mean of the dependent variable as the constant term of the
regression. There were 1409 families in the regression analysis.

age debt to income ratios in the middle income groups, especially for families with an income between $3,500 and $10,000 a year, but the changes are only very marginal and do not alter the rapidity with which installment debt use falls relative to income for families who had an average annual income of $10,000 or more.

Taking family life cycle into account does not alter the basic findings of Chapter 2. Other things equal, we cannot expect that the continued growth of income will be sufficient by itself to sustain the very rapid rate of expansion of consumer installment debt. If anything, real income gains would be expected to dampen the rate of growth of installment credit use over the longer-run. However, other things have not been constant. As shown in Chapter 2, the installment debt-income function shifted upward rapidly over the 15 years between 1955 and 1969 and the growth in credit use was especially marked among families who are relatively well-off. In any case the analysis does seem to make clear that, although continued prosperity and income growth may provide the basic consumer confidence necessary to stimulate the continued expansion of installment credit use, knowledge of the growth of income itself is probably one of the least important components of projections of future installment debt use. Of greater importance are the factors which have led to the upward shift in the installment debt function and the likelihood that the impact of these factors will continue to lead to further upward shifts in the near future.

Independent Impacts of Family Life Cycle

In the previous sections of this chapter we have been concerned with the impact of demographic characteristics on the relation between expenditures and income and between installment debt balances and income. We have been concerned particularly with the possibility that differences in family life cycle, if not taken properly into account, might substantially distort the income relations obtained from cross-sectional data. However, we have noted several times that family composition and life cycle characteristics have impacts on expenditure rates and on the use of installment credit beyond those associated with income level. In this section, we consider differences in expenditure rates on major durables and installment debt balances which are associated with family life cycle.

The regressions presented in Tables 4-3 and 4-5, which were used to examine differences in expenditure rates and installment debt use among income groups after adjusting for differences in family life cycle, may also be used to study the independent impact on expenditures and debt use of life cycle. As shown in Graph 4-1, the major differences in expenditure rates among family life cycle groups are accounted for by differences in marital status. Single people and single parent families all spend proportionately less of their income on consumer durables than do families with married heads. The dif-

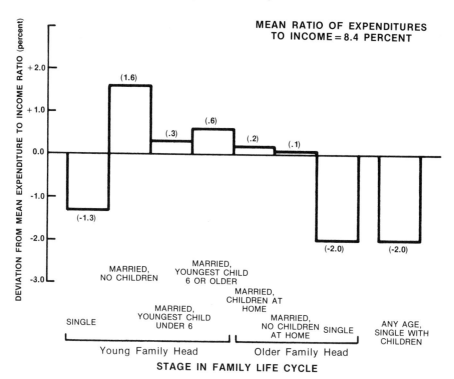

Graph 4-1
DEVIATION FROM MEAN EXPENDITURES AS A PROPORTION OF
INCOME BY STAGE IN FAMILY LIFE CYCLE AFTER ADJUSTMENT
FOR DIFFERENCES IN FAMILY INCOME

(ALL FAMILIES)

ference is especially striking for older people and single parent families where expenditure rates are 25 percent below the average for all families.

Among married couples, expenditure rates differ hardly at all, with the notable exception of families with young heads who had no children at the time of the first interview. Young, childless families spend from 1.0 to 1.5 percent more of their income on major consumer durables than do married couples at later stages in the family life cycle. Moreover, the expenditure rates of childless couples whose head was under age 45 would have been even higher if we included with them people who were single at the time of the first panel interview but who had married by the time of the last interview three years later. As shown in Table 4-3, after adjusting for other factors, panel families who got married after the time of the first interview spent an average of 11.6 percent of their income on consumer durables, or 3.2 percent more than average.[6]

That differences between expenditure rates exist primarily between married and single units supports the conclusion that shifts in the demand for durables arising from changes in the proportion and the number of American families in different stages of the family life cycle would occur only gradually over time. The size of the cohort, the members of which are coming of age in a particular period, will have some impact on the demand for durables. However, since all members of a cohort do not marry at the same age, even cohort effects should be spread out over a fairly long period of time and should have not very significant impacts on the total demand for durables, unless for some reason a cohort were very much smaller than the immediately older ones.

Family life cycle affects the use of installment debt much more dramatically than it does expenditures on major durables. Not only do married couples and single people differ, but among married couples there is a strong persistent decline in installment debt use as families move through the life cycle. As shown in Graph 4-2, young couples with no children clearly maintain the highest average outstanding installment debt balances with those who are very recently married, maintaining balances, on average, equal to 15 percent or more of their income (see Table 4-5). Higher than average balances are also maintained by younger families with children, but debt use declines as children get older. By the time the family head has reached age 45, the use of installment debt has fallen off considerably and falls to well below average for families whose children have left home.

Graph 4-2 clearly shows that changes in the proportion of American families at different stages in the family life cycle can be a powerful driving force in either accelerating or dampening the rate of growth of outstanding consumer installment credit. Indeed, the coming of age of the large cohort of the 1940's may well have been an important factor underlying the continued upward shift in the relation of outstanding installment debt to income during the late 1960's. Moreover, the data indicate that the rough estimates of the growth in installment credit, like those made by the credit industry, based only on the proportion of families who are within certain age groups, may be

---

[6]The early stages of the family life cycle are quite short for many people and changes in status within a period of three years are common. For example, of the 58 panel members who were single at the time of the first interview and completed the three reinterviews, 24 had married by the time of the final interview. Similarly, only half of the younger married couples with no children when interviewed in early 1967 still were childless when interviewed in early 1970.

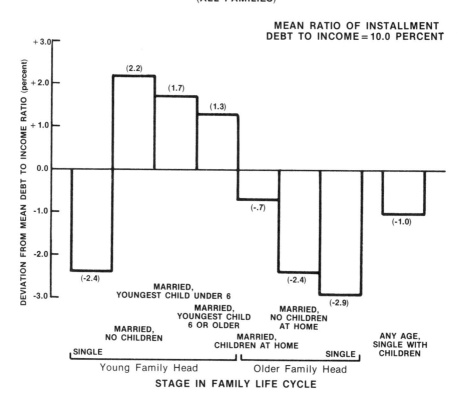

Graph 4-2
DEVIATION FROM MEAN OUTSTANDING INSTALLMENT DEBT TO
INCOME RATIO BY STAGE IN FAMILY LIFE CYCLE AFTER
ADJUSTMENT FOR DIFFERENCES IN FAMILY INCOME

(ALL FAMILIES)

very substantially in error. Trends in the age at which people marry, changes in the divorce rate, and the rapidity with which people remarry are all likely to be important in determing trends in installment credit use.

Housing Status

It is customary in studies of expenditures on major durables and the use of installment credit, to treat homeowners and renters separately.[7] The arguments most frequently given for studying homeowners and renters separately are that renters are likely to rent a substantial portion of their durables rather than own major durables outright, and secondly, that homeowners and renters are likely to be in very different wealth and asset positions. If renters do differ substantially in the amount of installment debt they use, or spend significantly less of their income than homeowners on major consumer durables, then the higher concentration of renters in the lower income groups could alter the income-expenditure and installment debt to income patterns observed in Chapter 2.

Looking at the gross differences in average annual expenditures on cars and major household durables, we find that those families classified as homeowners spent on the average slightly more than $900 per year. Renters, on the other hand, spent less than $600 per year. While the difference in absolute amounts spent is over $300, as shown at the bottom of Table 4-6, homeowners spent less than one percent more of their income on durables than did renters.

The larger expenditure rates on durables of families who are classified neither as homeowners nor as renters in Table 4-6, is probably due largely to the fact that these families were movers. It is well known that rates of expenditure on major durables by movers are generally larger than those for nonmovers.

As shown in Table 4-6, a large part of the discrepancy between homeowners and renters in expenditure rates is accounted for by low income renters who make up a substantial proportion of all renters and spend considerably less of their income on consumer durables than do lower income homeowners. As income rises, the differences between homeowners and renters disappear rapidly and there is no evidence that renters with an annual income of more than $10,000 spend less.

To some extent, Table 4-6 may exaggerate the difference in expenditures between homeowners and renters. Within the broad income groups shown, renters may have generally lower average incomes than do homeowners. This is especially likely to be true in the lowest income group. To control more carefully for the influence of the dissimilarity in the income distribution of

---

[7]See, for example, L. R. Klein, "Major Consumer Expenditures and Ownership of Durable Goods," *Bulletin of the Oxford University Institute of Statistics,* Vol. 17, No. 4, 1955; James N. Morgan, "Consumer Investment Expenditures," *The American Economic Review,* December, 1958; Harold W. Watts and James Tobin, "Consumer Expenditures and the Capital Account," *Proceedings of the Conference on Consumption and Saving,* Vol. 2, edited by Irwin Friend and Robert Jones, 1960.

Table 4-6

EXPENDITURE RATES ON MAJOR DURABLES OVER FOUR YEARS
WITHIN INCOME AND HOUSING STATUS GROUPS
(Cell Means and Frequencies)

Average Annual Income	All Families	Homeowners	Renters	Other, Change in Status
Less than $5,000	6.1 (191)	6.8 (67)	5.2 (80)	6.6 (44)
$5,000-9,999	9.2 (682)	9.0 (422)	8.5 (154)	10.6 (106)
$10,000-14,999	8.7 (383)	8.8 (308)	9.2 (39)	8.0 (36)
$15,000 or more	7.1 (150)	7.1 (134)	7.6 (5)	6.7 (11)
All Families	8.4 (1406)	8.5 (931)	7.7 (278)	9.0 (197)
Mean Income	$9,731	$10,793	$6,861	$9,657

NOTE: Numbers in parentheses are frequencies. Expenditure rates
are in percent.

renters and homeowners, a multiclassification analysis was carried out. In addition to housing status and average annual income, the regression also included the stage of the family life cycle of the head and changes in life cycle status.

As shown by the similarity of the adjusted and unadjusted deviations from mean expenditure rates in Table 4-7, taking other factors into account and adjusting for income in more detail does little to either increase or decrease the overall effect of housing status on expenditure rates. Moreover, including housing status in the analysis has no signifcant effect on the expenditure rates of either lower or higher income families beyond those effects which were already accounted for by the inclusion of life cycle.

A second analysis was run which included only families with incomes less than $10,000. Here again the differences between adjusted and unadjusted deviations among housing status groups were negligible, and the differential expenditure rates observed earlier among low income and high income groups again remained unaltered.

The lack of as substantial an impact of housing status on expenditures on cars and major household durables as is often assumed may be due to several factors. While it is true that some renters lease a major portion of their household durables, perhaps the proportion who actually do so is often exaggerated. In one recent Survey of Consumer Finances, for example, almost 85 percent of renters responded that they rented unfurnished quarters. Many of these families may consider accommodations which include basic kitchen durables as unfurnished. However, the percentage of unfurnished apartments where basic kitchen durables are provided may not be radically different from the percentage of owner-occupied homes which come so equipped.

Differential expenditure rates on consumer durables may also be reduced because of the way in which housing status is defined for the panel. Homeowners include all families who owned their own home at the time of the first and the last interview. Fifteen percent of these families moved between the beginning and the end of the panel, and some of these families rented in one or more intermediate years before acquiring a new home. These transitional renters would probably not be expected to spend very extensively on durables while they were in temporary quarters. However, in a single, non-reinterview survey, families in temporary rented quarters would be classified as renters and might possibly lower the average expenditure level for all renters.

The findings for installment debt use are in many ways similar to those for expenditure rates. As shown in Table 4-8, the ratio of average installment debt balances over four years to four-year income differs hardly at all between homeowners and renters when all families are taken together. Indeed, the difference is so small that one would be hard-pressed to assert at all that renters use less debt than homeowners. However, when families are divided

Table 4-7

RELATION OF HOUSING STATUS TO EXPENDITURE RATES
ON MAJOR DURABLES BEFORE AND AFTER ADJUSTMENT FOR DIFFERENCES
IN FAMILY INCOME

Predictors	Number of Families	Unadjusted Deviations	Adjusted Deviations
Average Annual Income (B^2=.029)			
Under $3,000	81	-2.9	-1.9
$3,000-4,999	110	-1.9	-1.1
$5,000-5,999	110	.7	.8
$6,000-7,499	195	1.1	1.2
$7,500-8,499	166	.7	.6
$8,500-9,999	211	.5	.2
$10,000-12,499	250	3.9	2.2
$12,500-14,999	133	1.9	- .1
$15,000-19,999	87	-1.0	-1.3
$20,000 or more	63	-1.7	-2.0
Housing Status (B^2=.003)			
Owner	931	.1	.1
Renter	278	-.7	-.6
Other, change in housing status	197	.6	.5

NOTE: The analysis also included stage in family life cycle and major
changes in life cycle. The dependent variable is the ratio (in percent) of expenditures on major durables to income over four years.
The mean of the dependent variable = 8.4 percent (constant term);
the R^2 for the regression is .058. Unadjusted deviations are
univariate subgroup means expressed as deviations from the sample
mean of 8.4. The adjusted deviations are dummy variable regression
coefficients under the constraint that the weighted sum of the set
of coefficients for a predictor equals zero. This yields the sample
mean of the dependent variable as the constant term of the regression. There were 1406 families in the regression analysis.

Table 4-8

RATIO OF INSTALLMENT DEBT TO INCOME OVER FOUR YEARS
WITHIN INCOME AND HOUSING STATUS GROUPS
(Cell Means and Frequencies)

Average Annual Income	All Families	Homeowners	Renters	Other, Change in Status
Less than $5,000	6.5 (197)	4.4 (68)	7.9 (87)	6.7 (42)
$5,000-9,999	12.0 (677)	11.5 (413)	10.7 (153)	14.4 (111)
$10,000-14,999	10.3 (386)	10.4 (310)	7.8 (39)	12.1 (37)
$15,000 or more	5.3 (149)	5.3 (133)	6.7 (5)	5.6 (11)
All Families	10.0 (1409)	9.7 (924)	9.0 (284)	12.3 (201)

NOTE: Numbers in parentheses are frequencies. Ratios of debt to income are in percent.

into broad income groups, there is some suggestion that families with roughly similar incomes do differ in the extent to which they use installment credit. As in the case of expenditure rates on major durables, the largest differences are between families with modest incomes and other families. Among families with an average annual income under $5,000, renters maintained installment balances relative to their income of about 8 percent, while homeowners maintained balances equal to less than 5 percent of their average annual income. At income levels of $5,000 or more, the impact of being a renter on installment debt balances relative to income is reversed. Among families in the $5,000 to $10,000 income group, installment debt balances relative to income are lower for renters than for homeowners, and it appears that at even higher income levels families who rent maintain lower installment debt balances than families who own their own home.

Since the impact of housing status on installment debt to income ratios is not consistent across all income groups, the effect of housing status on installment debt use and the relation between housing status and income cannot really be captured by a dummy variable regression analysis without including interaction terms. However, it is clear from Table 4-8 that the concentration of renters in the lower income groups does not contribute to the lower installment debt to income ratios found at the lower end of the income distribution. On the contrary, if anything, it is homeowners with very modest incomes who exert the greatest downward pull on debt use at low income levels.

In general, while there do appear to be some differences between homeowners and renters in the amounts of the income they spend on major consumer durables and the extensiveness of their use of installment debt, there is little evidence that differences in the observed relation between income and major expenditures, and income and installment debt use, are the result of differences in housing status *per se.* It also seems clear that controlling very carefully for differences in housing status would not contribute substantially to making the expenditure to income relation more nearly proportional across all income groups, nor would it change to any great extent the relationship between installment debt use and income observed in Chapter 2.

Chapter 5

INCOME CHANGE

A number of studies have used survey data to explore the responses of expenditures on major durables to movements in family income. In the early 1950's Klein, using British data, concluded that for moderate changes in income there is little discernable effect of income change on major discretionary expenditures.[1] Morgan, using a much larger sample and more refined techniques, concluded that "when people's incomes increase, they increase their expenditures on consumer investment items more than proportionately."[2] Both Morgan and Klein were looking at income changes over a period of one year.

Although Morgan's conclusion is very bold, and Klein's somewhat modest, the two sets of data show essentially the same thing: when large increases in income occur, families spend more than expected on major durables. Morgan estimates that for the period from 1947 to 1953, income changes of 25 percent or more over the course of a year were associated, on average, with expenditure rates about 2 percentage points higher than those expected on the basis of the housing status and stage in the family life cycle.

At first sight Morgan's conclusion may seem somewhat overstated since noticeable differences in responses are associated only with very substantial changes in income. However, a perusal of the early postwar data and more recent findings on short-run income variability from a study by Katona and Mueller put Morgan's findings into clearer perspective.

Using panel data collected at the time of the 1964 tax cut, George Katona and Eva Mueller examined in detail income changes over periods from four

---

[1] L. R. Klein, "Major Consumer Expenditures and Ownership of Durable Goods," *Bulletin of The Oxford University Institute of Statistics,* Volume 17, No. 4, 1955.

[2] James N. Morgan, "Consumer Investment Expenditures," *The American Economic Review,* December, 1958.

to six months.[3] Katona and Mueller found that in each of the three successive short periods approximately half of the family units had changes in income of more than 10 percent and that large income increases (greater than 20 percent) were consistently more frequent than smaller increases (10 to 19 percent). The study also presents convincing evidence that the amount of short-run income change observed is not the result of errors in reporting.[4]

In addition, Katona and Mueller's study distinguished income changes of greater and lesser durability. They isolated two types of income change which they call "sustainable" and "transitory" in order to avoid confusion with the broader time horizon variables proposed by Friedman and Modigliani. Making this distinction, Katona and Mueller found that sustainable income increases of 10 percent or more over brief periods of four to six months lead to substantial positive deviations from expected expenditure means in a multivariate analysis.[5] Families with favorable income developments which were classified as temporary also showed greater than average expenditures. The amounts by which their expenditures were greater than those expected, however, were much smaller. In addition, Katona and Mueller found that four to six months after the period in which the change in income was first reported, families with sustainable income increases still showed greater than expected expenditure levels.

Reference has been made here to only three studies. Responses of expenditures on consumer durables to short-run changes in income have also been examined by Janet Fisher, David S. Huang, De Min Wu, and others. The evidence from these studies all seems to point to the same conclusion: large changes in income are frequent and these changes, when positive, lead to larger than expected expenditures on consumer durable goods.

In this chapter we explore further the hypothesis that substantial upward adjustments in income lead to accelerated expenditure rates on major durables and that downward adjustments in income lead to lower rates of expenditure than would be expected on the basis of income alone.[6]

---

[3]George Katona and Eva Mueller, *Consumer Responses to Income Increases,* The Brookings Institution, Washington, D. C., 1969.

[4]Questions on sources of income variation revealed that over the entire 17 month period in which the three interviews were taken, nearly three-quarters of wage and salary earners had raises or cuts in pay. Other important sources of income variability were shown to include overtime pay, second jobs, job changes, unemployment, illness and the starting or stopping of work by the wife or some adult family member other than the head. On the basis of the data on sources of income variation, Katona and Mueller conclude that the "degree of income variability observed in these data is not greatly exaggerated by erratic reporting of incomes."

[5]Katona and Mueller used the multiple classification technique employed in Chapter 4 of this work.

[6]Because of the long debate regarding the permanent income and related hypotheses, the literature which focuses on the impact of income change as a major independent variable often

Measures of Income Trends

The work of Milton Friedman and others has made economists acutely aware of the multi-dimensionality of income change and the fact that households may respond differently to changes depending upon the source of the change, the time over which the new income level is expected to persist, and the certainty with which the household holds these expectations. The importance of taking separate account of at least some dimensions of income change, and understanding how the various dimensions interact and are perceived by households, is clearly demonstrated by the improved results obtained by Katona and Mueller when they took account, though crudely, of the difference between changes which are likely to be expected to persist and those which are likely to be reversed in the near future.

Two dimensions of income change are distinguished here: trends in income and the year-to-year variance of income around the trend. The distinction is made only for total family income after estimated federal income taxes. The various components of income which are changing are not taken into account.

In obtaining an adequate measure of the trend in a family's income over several years, one of the basic problems is developing a measure which is relatively free of the influence of unusually high or low incomes in the end years of the time-series. For example, a measure of the trend which simply took the difference in family income between 1966 and 1969 would be highly sensitive to any temporary deviation of income from normal in the end years of the panel because of such transitory phenomena as unemployment, short-term layoffs, more than usual overtime pay, illness, etc.

In an effort to minimize the impact of end-year transitory movements of income, an estimate of the income trend was obtained for each family in the panel by fitting a regression with total family income for each of the four years as the dependent variable and time as the single predictor of the series of incomes. The regressions were fit in two forms. First, income (Y) was made a linear function of time (t) and a constant term (a) and the regession $Y = a + bt$ was fit for each of the families in the panel. The estimate of "b" from this regression was used as a measure of the trend, the average change in income per year, to be used to predict expenditures and installment debt use. The same relation was estimated a second time for each family but with in-

---

appears to be quite muddled. In this chapter we focus almost exclusively on the issue of whether favorable income trends lead to accelerated rates of expenditure on major durables. It seems to us that this issue is qute distinct from any relating to the permanent income hypotheses. Regardless of whether the average and marginal propensities to save are the same, household decisions about whether to invest in durable goods, or to save in the form of financial assets, will have a considerable impact of the short-run level of economic activity.

come converted into logarithms to the base 10. Again "b" is the estimate of the trend in income but this time "b" is the percentage change in family income or, more precisely, the average annual compounded rate of income change.[7]

The distribution of percentage and dollar trends in income derived from the family-specific time series regressions are shown in Table 5-1. The average rate of income change for the panel as a whole was 7.8 percent. As we might expect, the rate of income growth (uncorrected for inflation) of panel families was somewhat higher than the rate of growth of disposable personal income for the household sector as a whole, which was between 7.3 and 7.5 percent. We would perhaps expect the general income experience of the panel to be somewhat better than that of the population as a whole, since older families were intentionally excluded from the panel, and panel losses tended to be somewhat more concentrated among families who were less optimistic about their probable financial progress.

The distribution of trends among families varied widely, as shown by the proportion of families who fall far on each side of the average trend value and by the standard deviation which is almost twice as large as the average rate of growth of income. For those families who had very substantial negative or positive trends in income, it is probably correct to think of these trends as an indication that years 1966 through 1969 were ones of transition to a new higher or lower income position that, once reached, will be maintained by these families with modest adjustments for some time in the future, rather than as trends in these families' incomes which are likely to be continued indefinitely into the future.

An examination of the trends in total family income among various population groups provides at least a weak test of the reasonableness of the estimates of the trends. Among life cycle groups the highest income trends are found amoung families with small children where the head is under 45 years of age (Table 5-2). Older married couples with no children under age 18 living at home and older single people have the lowest trends in income, with the average being only about half the average for the panel as a whole. Among

---

[7]Although using least squares techniques to estimate individual family income trends minimizes the impact on the trend of "abnormal" incomes in the first and last years of the panel, the effect of temporary deviations from the trend in income is not totally eliminated. In the family specific time series regressions, time takes on only four values, 1-4. Thus, the estimate of "b" in the time-series regressions reduces to:

$$b = \frac{3Y_{1969} + Y_{1968} - Y_{1967} - 3Y_{1966}}{10}$$

where the subscripts on income (Y) refer to the year in which the income was received. Hence, income received in the first and last years of the panel, 1966 and 1969, receives three times the weight of income received in the middle years of the panel in determining the trend in income.

Table 5-1

DISTRIBUTION OF INCOME TRENDS

(Percentage Distribution)

Income Trend (Dollars per Year)	Proportion of Families	Income Trend (Percent per Year)	Proportion of Families
-$500 or less	11	-10 percent or less	7
0 to -$499	11	-5.0 to -9.9	5
$1 to $249	10	0.0 to -4.9	10
$250 to $499	13	0.1 to 4.9	17
$500 to $999	20	5.0 to 9.9	22
$1,000 to $1,499	16	10.0 to 14.9	16
$1,500 or more	19	15.0 to 19.9	10
		20.0 percent or more	13
All Families	100	All Families	100

Table 5-2

INCOME TRENDS AMONG DEMOGRAPHIC GROUPS

Demographic Characteristic[1]	Mean Income Trend Trend in dollars	Rate of change	Proportion with: Declining or zero trend	Increasing trend of 15 Percent or more	Proportion of Families
Average Annual Income					
Less than $5,000	190	7.0	33	33	14
$5,000-9,999	590	7.8	21	22	49
$10,000-14,999	930	7.8	17	19	27
$15,000 or more	1,310	7.7	25	24	10
Marital Status					
Married all four years	750	7.6	20	21	79
Single all four years	290	5.5	30	20	12
Single to married	1,640	25.0	7	68	4
Married to single	-340	-3.6	57	15	4
More than one change in marital status	*	*	*	*	1
Stage in Family Life Cycle[2]					
Young, single	290	5.1	29	11	3
Young, married, no children	580	6.9	27	20	7
Young, married, youngest child under age 6	970	10.0	11	24	30
Young, married, youngest child 6 or older	900	8.7	16	21	15
Older, married, children at home	710	6.1	23	22	19
Older, married, no children at home	290	3.7	32	17	15
Older, single	240	3.7	31	14	6
Any age, single, with children	370	8.1	27	33	5

Table 5-2 (cont.)

Demographic Characteristic	Mean Income Trend		Proportion with:		Proportion of Families
	Trend in dollars	Rate of change	Declining or zero trend	Increasing trend of 15 percent or more	
Occupation of Head					
Professional, technical	1,010	9.8	17	22	14
Managers, officials (non-self-employed)	930	7.8	19	19	11
Self-employed businessmen and artisans	760	6.6	33	31	6
Clerical, sales	820	9.0	19	23	11
Craftsmen, foremen	770	8.3	16	19	19
Operatives	650	7.9	22	24	16
Laborers, service workers	490	6.9	23	24	10
Farmers, farm managers	130	2.5	46	29	4
Miscellaneous	680	13.0	27	35	4
Retired	-290	-10.1	37	25	5
All Families	700	7.8	.22	23	100
One standard deviation	1,540	15.8	-	-	-

*Too few families.

[1] Stage in family life cycle and occupation of the head at the time of the first interview in 1967.

[2] Includes only families where the head was either married or single all four years. Young families are those whose head was under age 45 in early 1967. Older families are those whose head was 45 to 59 in 1967.

these older families, declining trends are far more frequent than substantial upward trends.

The below average trends in income for young married couples who had no children at the time of the first interview may be somewhat deceiving. For many couples this stage in the family life cycle is very short. Of the 84 young married couples who had no children at the time of the first interview, 50 percent did have children three years later. These couples often had declines in total income because of reduced labor force participation of wives. Furthermore, the life cycle distribution shown includes only those families who were married all four years, or were single in all four years. As indicated by the tabulations by marital status, those individuals who married during the course of the panel generally had very large income increases, owing in part to the addition of an adult worker to the family unit.

While average income trends measured in dollars per year are highly correlated with average annual income, percentage income trends are not. A somewhat higher proportion of families with low average incomes were in the top or bottom two deciles of the distribution of income trends, indicating that significant movements in income, both up and down, are more common at the lower end of the income distribution. The panel data are not well suited to making generalizations about low income families. However, the greater proportion of families at the lower end of the income distribution, with both significant positive and significant negative movements in income over four years, would seem to indicate that movements into and out of that group of families—officially classified as the "poverty group"—may be more frequent than commonly believed.

The distribution of income trends seems highly reasonable for families with heads in different occupations. Professionals experience the highest average income gains. Income trends among blue-collar workers are closely related to skill level, with the more highly skilled groups experiencing larger average gains than the skilled groups beneath them. Although the panel includes only a few farmers, the experience of those in the panel was not encouraging. Almost half of them experienced a significant loss in real income. Significant income gains among farmers, however, were as common as were income gains in families with heads in other occupations.

Overall, the estimated trends in family income derived from the time series regressions for individual families seem to reflect reasonably what we might expect on the basis of the aggregate growth in personal income over the period 1966 through 1969, and the estimates seem to be in line with other information on the income experience of various demographic groups.

Measuring the Variance in Income

Based largely on the behavior of two special groups, farmers and self-employed businessmen, it has been asserted that families with greater income variability tend to save relatively more of their income. The argument is that uncertainty leads to an increased desire to maintain adequate reserve funds to sustain consumption activities during those times when income is below normal. *A priori*, there is no reason to argue strongly that income variance will affect expenditure rates on durable goods. On the one hand, a highly variable income might lead to investments in consumer durables which, once paid for, can be consumed at a fairly constant rate regardless of fluctuations in income. On the other hand, if saving in the form of financial assets is highly competitive with saving in the form of consumer durable assets, then increased income uncertainty might lead to lower expenditures on durables. Nevertheless, responses to income trends may be conditional upon the extent of variance around the trend. Also, income variance and the accompanying uncertainty may have a substantial impact on the use of installment debt.

Three measures of income variance were considered. The first was the proportion of variance in income left unexplained by the individual family unit regressions of income on time. The difficulty with the measure is that the correlation coefficients squared (R^2) from the regressions of income on time are strongly influenced by whether there is a trend in income. In cases where income varies around a nearly constant level, the explained variance (R^2) is close to zero and the unexplained variance $(1-R^2)$ close to one, regardless of how much income fluctuates from year to year.

A second index of relative income variability was calculated, which takes into account the ability of the regressions of income on time to explain mean income as well as the trend in income. For each family, the ratio of the sum of the predicted incomes squared to the sum of the actual incomes squared was calculated from the regression of income on time for that family. Preliminary tabulations of this measure, however, showed that it was very insensitive and yielded similar values for all families except those with the most extreme variations in income. The possible range of values the ratio can take on are 0.0 to 1.0. For more than 80 percent of the families the value actually calculated lay in the range between .80 and .99.

A final measure was constructed which is more sensitive than the ratio of the sum of the squared predicted incomes to the sum of actual incomes squared, and unlike the R^2, does not depend upon the strength of the relationship between income and time. The sum of the absolute values of the differences between predicted and actual income for each year was divided by the total disposable income of the family over the entire four years. The variance then becomes relative to the level of income and can be conveniently expressed as a percentage. For a given dollar amount of variance around the income trend line, the actual value of the measure will be inversely related to the level of income of the family. For a family with an average income of $5,000 and annual deviations from the fitted trend line of about $1,000 in each of the years, the variance in family income will be about 20 percent. For a family with an average income of $10,000 and variance around the trend of about $1,000 in each year, the variance in family income will be only about 10 percent.

The income variance measure is not entirely unbiased since variance is measured from a trend which is by definition linear. For example, the income of a family may rise steadily with no setback over several years, but unless income increases by exactly the same amount each year, the variance around a linear approximation of the trend in income will be greater than zero. Hence, there is a bias toward greater variance in income than families may in fact experience. To take an extreme case, assume that two families have incomes in the first year of the panel (1966) of $10,000 and in the last year (1969) $13,000. Further, suppose that for the first family the entire change in income occurs during the second year of the panel, so that its annual income is $10,000 in 1966 and $13,000 thereafter. For the second family suppose that the movement from an income of $10,000 to $13,000 occurs by annual increments of $1,000 in each successive year. In the case of the first family the variance of income around a linearly approximated trend for the whole period will be quite large. In the case of the second family the variance around the linearly approximated trend is zero. Yet, the first family experienced little or no variation in its income over the period and certainly no more than the second family.

The distribution of the variance of income around the linear approximation of the trend in income of the individual families is shown below:

Variance in Income	Proportion of Families
Less than 2.5 percent	13
2.5-4.9 percent	21
5.0-7.4 percent	17
7.5-9.9 percent	12
10.0-14.9 percent	15
15.0-19.9 percent	9
20.0-29.9 percent	8
30.0 or greater	5
All Families	100

After the trend in income is taken into account, the variance in income is less than that implied on the basis of calculations of differences which do not take trends into account. Despite the reduction in the overall variation in income, however, the relative variance between demographic groups is consistent with the findings of others.[8] For self-employed businessmen and farmers, income variance is high relative to the average experience of families with heads in other occupations (Table 5-3). Families with heads who were retired at the beginning of the panel, or who were in the miscellaneous group, also had higher than average fluctuations in income. Families headed by lesser-skilled blue collar workers are above average in the amount of income variance they experience, though not so far above average as the self-employed group. The less skilled are doubtless more vulnerable to unemployment, and such factors as the availability of overtime work may loom large in determinint their income over fairly short periods. Among income groups, families with an average income below $5,000 have by far the most variable incomes.

Several groups are notable for the stability of their income. Nearly half of the families headed by professionals and managers had income paths which deviated but little from their trends, and the relative variance in income was lower for these groups than for any others in the occupational distribution. Also, families with an average income between $10,000 and $15,000 were particularly unlikely to have fluctuations in income which equaled or exceeded 15 percent of their disposable income over the period, after the trend in income was removed. There is no obvious reason why families in this particular income group should experience extreme variations in income so much less frequently than other families.

On the whole, the distributions in Tables 5-2 and 5-3 present fairly convincing evidence that using simple regressions to calculate a family's income trend over a period of four years is a fairly good first approximation of the path of income for a large number of families. From a substantive point of view, the lower variance found in income after the trend in income has been accounted for, implies that a fairly large proportion of the year-to-year income variance observed by others represents permanent changes in income status. Moreover, the measure of income variance presented in Table 5-2, while it may contain much random variation, does corroborate the findings of past studies, and appears, on the surface at least, to capture the variability dimension of income change.

Income Change and Expenditures

In column (1) of Table 5-4, expenditures on major durables as a proportion of income over the last three years of the panel are related to income trends over that same period. While earlier studies have shown repeatedly that increases in income, especially increases that are likely to be sustained, lead to

---

[8]See for example, Ralph B. Bristol, Jr. "Factors Associated with Income Variability," *American Economic Review Papers and Proceedings,* May, 1958 and George Katona and Janet Fisher, "Postwar Changes in the Income of Identical Consumer Units," *Studies in Income and Wealth,* Vol. 13, 1951.

Table 5-3

INCOME VARIANCE AMONG DEMOGRAPHIC GROUPS

Demographic Characteristic[1]	Mean Deviation from Income Trend		Proportion with:	
	Sum of deviations (dollars)	Variance relative to income (percent)	Variance under 5 percent	Variance of 15 percent or more
Average Annual Income				
Less than $5,000	2165	17.6	18	49
$5,000-9,999	3027	10.1	33	21
$10,000-14,999	3631	7.5	41	10
$15,000 or more	8481	9.3	38	20
Marital Status				
Married all four years	3541	9.2	37	29
Single all four years	2562	12.4	30	18
Single to married	4273	16.7	9	41
Married to single	6144	16.1	12	43
More than one change in marital status	*	*	*	*
Stage in Family Life Cycle[2]				
Young, single	2191	7.9	45	16
Young, married, no children	3746	10.0	35	26
Young, married, youngest child under 6	3256	8.8	40	17
Young, married, youngest child 6 or older	3264	7.9	38	11
Older, married, children at home	4127	10.3	34	23
Older, married, no children at home	3547	9.6	34	17
Older, single	2349	12.3	35	30
Any age, single with children	3069	14.9	15	37
Occupation of Head				
Professional, technical	3922	7.8	45	14
Managers, officials (non-self-employed)	4672	7.7	44	11
Self-employed businessmen and artisans	5974	14.4	12	40
Clerical, sales	3085	8.3	41	14
Craftsmen, foremen	3117	8.4	35	13
Operatives	2901	9.5	38	18
Laborers, service workers	2775	12.5	26	32
Farmers, farm managers	5335	17.8	14	44
Miscellaneous groups	4292	18.8	12	60
Retired	3044	17.5	15	44
All Families	3638	10.4	34	22

*Too few families.

[1] Stage in family life cycle and occupation of head are at the time of the first interview in 1967.

[2] Includes only families where the head was either married or single all four years. Young families are those whose head was under age 45 in early 1967. Older families are those whose head was 45 to 59 in 1967.

Table 5-4

THREE-YEAR RATIO OF EXPENDITURES ON DURABLES TO INCOME
WITHIN INCOME TREND GROUPS
(Class Means)[1]

Income Trend (Dollars per year)	All Families	Under $5,000	$5,000– 9,999	$10,000– 14,999	$15,000 or more
-$500 or less	7.9	7.0	8.4	7.6	7.7
0 to -$499	7.6	6.2	7.8	8.8	9.4**
$1 to 249	7.3	4.9	8.1	8.7	7.5**
$250 to 499	8.3	6.5	9.3	6.9	13.1**
$500 to 999	8.2	7.1	8.7	7.7	6.5**
$1,000 to 1,499	9.0	7.7*	9.5	9.2	7.7
$1,500 or more	8.6	–	9.7	8.8	7.3
Income Trend (Percent per year)					
-10.0 percent or less	7.0	5.8	7.6	7.5*	8.0
-5.0 to -9.9	8.0	4.7*	9.7	6.7*	7.0**
Zero to -4.9	8.0	7.1	7.8	9.0	7.8
0.1 to 4.9	7.7	6.9	8.0	7.5	8.1
5.0 to 9.9	8.2	5.6	9.0	8.3	7.2
10.0 to 14.9	8.3	5.2*	9.1	8.4	7.2
15.0 to 19.9	9.3	9.3*	10.1	9.0	7.8
20.0 percent or more	8.7	6.2	9.5	9.5	7.9
All Families	8.2	6.3	8.8	8.4	7.6
Number of Families	1406	191	631	420	164

---

[1]Ratios are in percent.

*Cell contains fewer than 20 families

**Cell contains fewer than 10 families.

increased expenditures on major discretionary items, there is only a modest relation between trends in income over three years and expenditure rates on cars and major household durables. To be sure, income trends do seem to have some slight influence. For example, families whose general trend in income was downward spent an average of less than 8 percent of their income on major durables, while families whose income was rising an average of $1,000 a year or more spent about 9 percent of their income on major durables.

When percentage changes in income are considered, the results are unchanged. Families with highly favorable trends tend to spend somewhat more of their income on consumer durables, and those with unfavorable trends somewhat less. The fact remains, however, that families with vastly different trends in income differ hardly at all in the proportion of income they allocate to investments in consumer durables.

Income trends, whether computed as average dollar or average percentage rates of growth, do not necessarily mean the same thing to families at different income levels. At very low incomes, for example, large percentage changes may occur without adding significantly to the discretionary income of the family, while at relatively high incomes even small percentage changes may add substantially to the discretionary income of the family. To control for the possibility that responses to income change may be obscured because the trend measures do not have the same meaning at all levels of income, the panel was divided into 4 broad income groups, and the relation of expenditure rates to income trends was examined within each. The results are shown in columns (2) through (5) of Table 5-4.

Even after controlling for income level, there are few discernible differences in the average expenditure rates among families with widely different trends in income. Moreover, there is only very slight evidence that families at different income levels respond differently to such trends. Each income group up to $15,000 or more shows some very slight response to trends in income. For families with an average income of $15,000 or more, however, there is no evidence of even modest differences in expenditure rates among income trend groups.

The influence of income trends on consumer durable expenditures is explored using ordinary least squares regressions in Table 5-5. Regressions (2) and (3) look at expenditures on major durables as a continuous, linear and additive function of average annual income over the last three years of the panel, income squared and income trend. The coefficients, both on percentage and on dollar trends, are not only very small but both are also statistically insignificant. Also, adding income trends in the regression of expenditures on income and income squared—equation (1) in Table 5-5—does not increase the proportion of variance in expenditures explained. The first three regressions in Table 5-5 further reinforce the conclusion that income trends

Table 5-5

REGRESSIONS OF THREE-YEAR AVERAGE EXPENDITURES ON THREE-YEAR
AVERAGE ANNUAL INCOME AND INCOME TREND

(All Families)

Regression Number	Constant	Average Annual Income	Income Squared	Income Trend (Dollars)	Income Trend (Percent)	Income Variance	R^2
				Regression Coefficients			
(1)	−74	.107 (17.7)	.000001 (9.2)	−	−	−	.275
(2)	−79	.108 (17.3)	.000001 (9.2)	.010 (0.9)	−	−	.276
(3)	−77	.106 (17.5)	.000001 (9.0)	−	1.40 (1.3)	−	.276
(4)	−128	.111 (17.1)	.000001 (9.3)	−.009 (0.8)	−	2.78 (1.6)	.278
(5)	−128	.109 (17.2)	.000001 (9.2)	−	1.44 (1.3)	2.86 (1.6)	.278

NOTE: The numbers in parentheses below the slope coefficients are
t-ratios. Each regression includes 1406 families.

over several years have almost no influence on expenditures on major durables beyond the impact which the trends have on average annual income itself.

It is possible that the influence of income trends on expenditure is not straightforward, but is conditional upon other things. Katona has stressed that it is *repeated* favorable changes which are most important in stimulating discretionary spending. At least one possibility, then, is that responses depend upon the amount of variance in income around the trend.

As shown in regressions (4) and (5) in Table 5-5, the addition of income variance has no effect on either of the income trend variables. The magnitude of the impact of income trend on expenditures remains small and, as indicated by the t-ratios, there is no change in the standard errors.

In addition, the assertion made earlier in this chapter that there is no *a priori* reason to expect that greater income variability will lead systematically to either more or less spending on major consumer durable goods, seems to be borne out. In regressions (4) and (5) the coefficients on relative income variance are less than twice their standard errors. In both cases they are also positive, suggesting (at least within the simple regression framework used here) that increased income variability tends to lead to slightly greater spending. The coefficients imply that each percentage point increase in income variance is associated with an increase in average annual expenditures on durables of slightly less than $3.

In addition to simply adding income variance to equations (2) and (3), the regressions were run separately for families with larger and smaller amounts of income variance (less than 5 percent, 5 to 14.9 percent, and 15 percent or more). The regressions (not presented here) for each of the income variance subgroups revealed no noteworthy differences in responses to income trends.

Before finally concluding that income trends over several years do not lead to accelerated rates of expenditure on major durables, one final experiment was carried out. Research by others suggests that responses to increasing and decreasing trends are not symmetric. Morgan, for example, found asymmetric responses in the study referred to earlier in this chapter. After adjusting for a number of situational variables—family life cycle, age, and housing status—Morgan examined the deviations of ratios of current expenditures to current income from those expected by change in family income over the past year. For families whose incomes increased by 25 percent or more, Morgan found positive deviations in rates of expenditure. He also found positive deviations for families whose income declined by 25 percent or more over the past year.

Morgan, of course, was examining income change over one year only and relating that change to expenditures which occurred within the same year. The higher than expected rates of expenditure on durables found among families with substantial income declines may only indicate that in a particular year many income declines are perceived as temporary setbacks rather than permanent changes in income status. Moreover, preliminary findings from more recent data, collected as a part of a five-year panel specifically designed to study the dynamics of income change, indicate that declines in income are frequently unexpected, while income increases are often anticipated.[9] Unexpected income declines might well lead to observed expenditure rates in one-year data that are higher than expected since the purchase of a major durable may have preceded the actual decline in income. Whether such lags would persist when the general trend is downward is questionable.

Although the data in Table 5-4 do not indicate strong asymmetry in responses to income trends, separate regressions were run for families with favorable trends in income and for families with unfavorable trends. Since the cost of living rose substantially over the years between 1966 and 1969, an income trend of 4.5 percent per year was chosen as the arbitrary dividing line between families with rising and families with declining trends in income. Moreover, since in regression analysis extreme cases may affect substantially the estimated slope coefficients and we felt that average trends in income of 25 percent or more may lie outside the reliable range of the income trend variables, families whose income trends exceeded 25 percent in either direction were excluded. The regressions for families with favorable and for families with unfavorable trends are shown below:

Favorable trends:

$$(1) \ E = -68 + .107 \ Y - .000002 \ Y2 + .047 \ dY/dt$$
$$ (10.6) (6.3) (1.1)$$

$$R2 = .237$$
$$N = 755$$

Unfavorable trends:

$$(2) \ E = -91 + .101 \ Y - .000001 \ Y2 - .030 \ dY/dt$$
$$ (10.4) (5.6) (0.9)$$

$$R2 = .274$$
$$N = 501$$

where E is average annual expenditures for the last three years of the panel, Y is average annual income over the same period, and dY/dt is the trend in income in dollars per year. N is the number of families in each regression.

---

[9]For a detailed description of the data available from Morgan's five-year panel study see *A Panel Study of Income Dynamics: Study Design, Procedures, Available Data. 1968-1971 Interviewing Years.* The Institute for Social Research, Ann Arbor, Michigan, 1971.

Looking at families with favorable income trends separately increases the magnitude of the impact of favorable trends on expenditures. Moreover, the negative sign on the coefficient of income trend in equation (2), implying that decreases in income increase expenditures on major durables, does suggest that there is either some lag in families' adjustments to permanent declines in income, or that downward adjustments in income, even ones that are expected to persist, are largely unexpected. However, for both families with favorable and families with unfavorable trends, the coefficients on income trend, being less than twice their standard errors, are not signifcantly different statistically from zero. Even if income trend were statistically significant, the coefficients imply that expenditures would only change by four cents for each dollar of change in income trend.

Other analyses were also tried. Both ordinary least squares and dummy variable regression analyses were performed which took account of other factors which might influence responses to income trends. Subgroup regressions were run within age groups, and in addition, family life cycle and occupation were adjusted for. In none of these additional analyses could any substantial evidence be found that trends in family income, even vastly different trends, lead to increases in expenditures that were more rapid than the increases in income, or declines in expenditures that were either more rapid or substantially less rapid than declines in income.

Income Change and Installment Debt

It is incorrect to assume that because income trends do not lead to accelerated rates of investment in consumer durables, that they will also have no effect upon outstanding installment debt balances. As shown in Table 5-6, average ratios of installment debt to income ratios over the last three years of the panel are higher for families with increasing trends in income than for families whose incomes were generally declining. For example, the 101 panel families who experienced declines in income of 10 percent or more per year maintained installment debt balances equal to about 6 percent of their average annual income. Families with average income increases of 10 percent or more each year, on the other hand, maintained installment debt balances of from 10 to about 12 percent of their income.

Dividing families into two groups on the basis of average annual income shows that the influence of trends in income on installment debt use is stronger and that the changes from one income trend group to another are more consistent for families with an average annual income of less than $10,000, than for higher income families. Even for higher income families, however, income trends do seem to make some difference.

In Table 5-7 regressions have been run separately for families with average annual incomes of less than $10,000 and families with incomes of $10,000 or more. Separate regressions are shown using income trends measured in dol-

Table 5-6

THREE-YEAR RATIO OF OUTSTANDING INSTALLMENT DEBT TO INCOME
WITHIN INCOME TREND GROUPS

(Cell Means and Percentage Distributions)

Income Trend (Percent Per Year)	All Families Ratio of Debt to Income	Average Income Under $10,000		Average Income $10,000 or More	
		Ratio of Debt to Income	Proportion of Families	Ratio of Debt to Income	Proportion of Families
-10 percent or less	6.1	6.7	9	3.8	4
-5.0 to -9.9	8.1	8.2	7	7.5	3
0.0 to -4.9	9.9	9.5	10	10.5	10
.1 to 4.9	9.2	10.1	18	7.9	16
5.0 to 9.9	9.7	11.1	19	8.0	24
10.0 to 14.9	11.6	12.0	14	11.2	19
15.0 to 19.9	11.4	12.9	9	9.8	11
20.0 percent or more	10.2	10.1	14	10.5	13
All Families	9.8	10.3	100	9.2	100
Number of Families	1404	—	823	—	581

Table 5-7

REGRESSIONS OF THREE-YEAR AVERAGE OUTSTANDING INSTALLMENT DEBT
ON THREE-YEAR AVERAGE ANNUAL INCOME AND INCOME TREND

Dependent Variable	Constant	Average Annual Income	Income Trend (Dollar)	Income Trend (Percent)	R^2
Income Under $10,000					
(1) Three-Year Average Debt	−172	.150 (10.1)	−	−	.109
(2) Three-Year Average Debt	−162	.130 (10.7)	.087 (3.0)	−	.156
(3) Three-Year Average Debt	−179	.143 (9.7)	−	7.41 (3.5)	.121
(4) Debt to Income Ratio	10.9	−	.002 (4.3)	−	.022
(5) Debt to Income Ratio	11.0	−	−	.107 (3.4)	.014
Income of $10,000 or more					
(6) Three-Year Average Debt	1261	.001 (0.1)	−	−	.000
(7) Three-Year Average Debt	1245	−	.027 (0.9)	−	.001
(8) Three-Year Average Debt	1204	.001 (0.1)	−	6.04 (1.4)	.004
(9) Debt to Income Ratio	14.6	−.0004 (5.1)	.0003 (1.4)	−	.044
(10) Debt to Income Ratio	13.6	−.0003 (5.2)	−	.055 (2.0)	.051

NOTE: The numbers in parentheses below the slope coefficients are t-ratios.

lars per year and using percentage rates of growth of income as independent variables. In addition, the regressions were run using the ratio of installment debt balances to income as well as the average level of outstanding installment debt.

For families with an income of under $10,000 a year in the last three years of the panel, all of the coefficients on income trend, whether measured in percent per year or dollars per year, are more than three times as large as their standard errors. Not only is income trend a statistically significant predictor of outstanding installment debt balances, but the inclusion of income trend in the regression substantially increases the proportion of variance in installment debt balances explained. Comparing the R^2 of regression (1) in Table 5-7, which does not include income trend as a predictor, with the R^2 of equation (2), which includes income trend, shows that the addition of the income trend increases the explained variance in average installment debt balances by almost 5 percent.

Since, as shown in Table 5-6, the relation of installment debt to income trend is nearly linear for families with an income of less than $10,000, the slope coefficients on income trend in Table 5-7 should be reasonably good estimates of the magnitude of the impact of income trend on debt use. According to regression (2), each change of one dollar in the income trend of a family in the under $10,000 income group leads, on average, to an increase in outstanding installment debt balances of nine cents. Thus, for a family whose income increased on average by $500 each year over the last three years of the panel, we would expect the installment debt balances maintained by the family to be about $45 higher than the balances maintained by a family whose income was constant.

A set of regressions similar to those for families with an income less than $10,000 are shown in the bottom half of Table 5-7 for families with average incomes of $10,000 or more. These regressions confirm the finding that income trends influence the installment debt use of higher income families far less than for families at low or moderate income levels. The slope coefficients on income trend are all very small, and none is more than twice its standard error.

The lack of any strong systematic impact of income trend on the debt balances of upper and upper-middle income families is not surprising considering the relationship between installment debt and income observed in Chapter 2. There it was shown that families with an income of $10,000 or more tend to maintain the same average level of outstanding installment debt, regardless of their relative position in the upper part of the income distribution.

In an earlier section of this chapter we suggested that, although there were no strong reasons to expect income variance to influence greatly expenditures on major durables, it seemed probable that families whose income fluctuates widely would be less inclined to maintain installment balances that were high relative to their income than would families whose income is either stable or follows a fairly stable trend. An extensive examination of the relation of income variation to installment debt use was not conducted. However, a preliminary set of regressions was run for families with average incomes of less than $10,000 a year, and whose trends in income did not exceed 25 percent per year in either direction. One of these regressions, which shows the ratio of installment debt balances to income (D/Y) as a function of the trend in income (YTRD) in percent per year and income variance (YVAR) as a percent of average income, is presented below:

$$(3) \ D/Y = 10.6 + .099 \ YTRD - .088 \ YVAR$$
$$\quad\quad\quad\quad\quad (2.7) \quad\quad\quad\quad (2.4)$$

$$R^2 = .018$$
$$N = 760$$

where N is the number of families included in the analysis.

As expected, the sign of the coefficient on income variance is negative, indicating that increases in the variance of income decreases the amount of outstanding installment debt balances maintained as a proportion of income. Moreover, the coefficient on income variance is more than twice its standard error.

While the above regression clearly indicates that the influence of income stability on debt use is in the expected direction, it must be noted that the magnitude of the impact is quite small. According to the regression, each increase in variance relative to income of 1 percentage point leads to a decrease in installment debt balances relative to income of slightly less than one-tenth of a percentage point. It is possible that the impact of income fluctuations would have been larger had a more refined measure of income variance been developed.

Chapter 6

PERCEPTIONS OF FINANCIAL PROGRESS

In the previous chapter we examined the relation of major expenditures on consumer durables and the use of installment credit to changes in income, as computed by comparing family income reported in successive years. There we found that trends in income do not lead to rates of expenditure on major durables over three years that are either higher or lower than those of other families with the same average income level but with greatly different income trends. These findings imply that, although replacements and expansions of stocks of consumer durables are likely to follow favorable changes in income, these changes only represent the normal change in the demand for durables associated with having either a higher or a lower income. Thus, over the historical period of the panel at least, there is little evidence that rapid growth in personal income led to accelerated rates of expenditure. Income trends were shown to have an impact on outstanding installment debt balances for families with an income under $10,000. However, the estimated magnitude of the impact was relatively small.

Trends in income are but one dimension of income change. Yet another is the way in which families perceive these changes and their expectations regarding future changes in income and financial well-being. In this chapter we examine the cumulative impact over four years of perceptions of changes in personal financial situation, and expectations regarding future change.

The analysis in this chapter differs from traditional studies of the relation of attitudes and expectations to discretionary transactions in two respects. First, in the past change in attitudes has most often been correlated with aggregate behavior in order to test the proposition that a change in the sentiment of all consumers would have an impact on their total expenditures on durables and on the aggregate change in debt incurrence. In this chapter, attitudes are related directly to the behavior of the individual family holding those attitudes. Second, in the past, when the relation of individual attitudes has been studied, the studies have been limited to behavior over short periods only.

Construction of an Index

In each of the four successive annual interviews, respondents were asked the question, "Would you say that you and your family are better off, or worse off financially than you were a year ago?" Regarding the future, people were asked, "Do you think that a year from now you people will be better off financially or worse off, or just about the same as now?" To construct an index, the responses to these two questions were combined for each year, giving equal weight to evaluations of past financial progress and to expected future progress. Responses of "better off" to either question were assigned a value of +1, responses of "worse off" a value of -1. Responses of "same" and "don't know" were assigned a value of 0. Thus, for one year families who felt that they were better off than they were a year ago and expected to be better off in the future received 2 points. At the other extreme, families who felt that they were worse off financially than a year ago and expected that during the course of the next year their financial position would deteriorate still further received a score of -2.

For each family the scores of the individual years were summed across all four years. The distribution of scores is shown below:

Index Score	Proportion of Families	Number of Families
-4 to -6	2	24
-3	2	35
-2	4	61
-1	6	86
0	12	168
1	11	158
2	12	174
3	12	166
4	11	151
5	10	148
6	8	114
7	6	88
8	4	63
Total	100	1436

Although the possible range of scores is from +8, for families who felt that they were better off each year and would become still better off during the next year, to -8, for families who felt that their financial position had deteriorated and would to continue to deteriorate in the near future, the actual range of scores is only from +8 to -6. Moreover, relatively few of the families in the panel were highly pessimistic about recent developments in their financial situation, while many evaluated their financial progress optimistically most of the time.

Subjective Financial Progress and Expenditures

Attitudes toward past and expected financial progress do influence the proportion of income spent on major consumer durables. As shown in Table 6-1, almost half of the families with highly negative evaluations of their year-to-year financial progress and their prospects for the near future devoted less than 5 percent of their income to investments in major durables. Yet among even moderately optimistic families, only one-quarter spent as little as 5 percent of their income on durables, and still fewer families with highly optimistic evaluations of their progress spent so little.

Although optimism regarding the financial progress of the family clearly encourages families to spend at least moderate proportions of their income on major consumer durables, differences in optimism alone seem insufficient to encourage unusually high expenditures. Expenditures on major durables of as much as 15 percent of income were no more frequent among moderately optimistic families than among moderately pessimistic families. Only in the extreme groups—those who were highly pessimistic or highly optimistic—does the proportion of those who spent 15 percent or more of their income on major durables differ significantly from the proportion of all families who spent that much.[1]

The general trend indicated in Table 6-1 becomes even clearer when mean expenditure rates are considered. In Graph 6-1 the mean proportion of income allocated to purchases of major durables is shown for families with differing evaluations of their financial progress. The modal group of families (including 35 percent of all families) are those with index scores in the range from +1 to +3. This group is made up primarily of families who only in one or two of the four years reported or expected an improvement in their financial situation and in the other years reported no change. The average proportion of income spent on durables by this group of families was 8.4 percent, the same as that for all panel families. Families who were more optimistic than the middle group spent more, and those who were less optimistic spent less. Graph 6-1 also suggests that the effect on expenditures of being relatively less optimistic than average is stronger than the effect of being somewhat

---

[1]Pessimism appears to have a stronger dampening effect on expenditures than optimism had an accelerating effect. This may reflect the general state and change in attitudes over the particular historical period of the panel. While many families felt good about their own financial situation, they were not generally optimistic about business conditions. This may have dampened responses to optimism regarding personal financial progress.

Table 6-1

FOUR-YEAR RATIO OF DURABLE EXPENDITURES TO INCOME RELATED TO
EVALUATION OF FINANCIAL PROGRESS
(Percentage Distribution)

Four-Year Ratio of Expenditures to Income	All Families	Evaluation of Financial Progress						
		Highly Pessimistic (Score -3 to -6)	Score -1 to -2	Score of 0	Score 1 to 3	Score 4 to 5	Score 6 to 7	Highly Optimistic (Score of 8)
Less than 5.0 percent	29	47	37	31	32	22	26	11
5.0-9.9 percent	33	29	27	33	31	35	35	46
10.0-14.9 percent	23	17	23	22	21	28	25	21
15.0 percent or more	15	7	13	14	16	15	14	22
Total	100	100	100	100	100	100	100	100
Proportion of Families	100	4	10	12	35	21	14	4

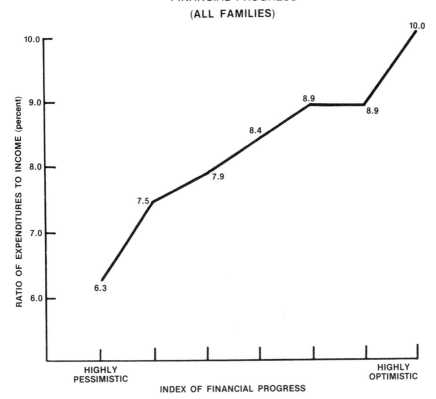

Graph 6-1
MEAN FOUR-YEAR RATIO OF EXPENDITURES ON MAJOR
DURABLES TO FAMILY INCOME BY PAST AND EXPECTED
FINANCIAL PROGRESS
(ALL FAMILIES)

more optimistic. Among families who were more optimistic than average, only those who reported consistent, uninterrupted past and expected gains differ markedly from the modal group.

Even though financial progress as measured here does not bear a completely linear relation to expenditures on major durables, the relation is close enough to justify a linear approximation of the response. For purposes of comparison, the first regression shown in Table 6-2 includes only average annual income and income squared as predictors of expenditures on durables. In regression (2) the index of financial progress is added.

As shown by the t-ratio on attitudes in regression (2), the coefficient on the index is more than three times its standard error, indicating that felt financial progress is a statistically significant predictor of major expenditures when income is taken into account simultaneously. According to regression (2), each point on the index represents an average change in expenditures of about $17. Thus, the implied difference in expenditures across the whole range of actual values of the index (-6 to +8) is over $200 per year. That the difference is substantial is clear when it is recalled that average annual expenditures on durables for the panel was only slightly over $800.

Despite the sizeable impact of attitudes regarding personal financial progress on purchases of consumer durables, the adjusted R^2 for regression (1) in Table 6-2, which does not include the index, is practically the same as for regression (2) which does. The small difference no doubt reflects the inability of the index to differentiate well between the many families in its middle range, where a large number of combinations of better off, same, and worse off, yield approximately the same score. A better scaling of the index might perhaps increase the amount of variance in expenditures explained.

In the bottom section of Table 6-2, the sample is divided into several groups in order to examine the consistency of responses to perceived and expected financial progress at different levels of income. This is especially important since the index and income are correlated.[2] As shown by the similarity of the coefficients in regressions (3)-(8), the estimate based on all families is representative of the responsiveness of expenditures to perceptions of financial progress, regardless of the income group to which a family belongs. The constancy of response in terms of dollars, of course, indicates that, relative to income, responses are greater at lower and middle income levels than at higher income levels.

Income is not the only variable that is correlated with evaluations of financial progress. As shown in Table 6-3, the degree of optimism which families hold regarding their past and expected financial progress is closely associated with the age of the family head and with the stage in the family life cycle. Among families whose head was under age 45 at the beginning of the panel, fully 25 percent felt each time they were interviewed that their financial situation had improved over the past year and they expected that it would continue to improve over the forthcoming year. Among families whose head was over age 45, on the other hand, only about half as large a proportion felt that their financial situation was consistently improving and expected it to continue to improve. Indeed, pessimism among the panel families ran very high among older families and was especially prominent among older single people, over 50 percent of whom had negative scores on the index.

---

[2] Almost a third of the families with an average annual income of under $5,000 were pessimistic both about the financial progress they were making and about the progress they expected to make in the near future. On the other hand, only 8 percent of the families with an income of $15,000 or more per year were pessimistic about the changes in their financial situation. At the other end of the continuum, the proportion of families with highly optimistic outlooks rose substantially with income, increasing from 6 percent at an income of under $5,000 a year to 30 percent at an income of $15,000 or more per year.

Table 6-2

REGRESSIONS OF AVERAGE ANNUAL DURABLE EXPENDITURES ON INDEX OF PAST AND EXPECTED FINANCIAL PROGRESS AND AVERAGE ANNUAL INCOME

Income Group	Regression Coefficients				R^2	Number of Families
	Constant Term	Average Annual Income	Average Income Squared	Index of Financial Progress		
All Families						
(1)	-37	.105 (20.8)	-.0000013 (11.3)	—	.324	1406
(2)	-48	.101 (19.6)	-.0000013 (10.7)	16.7 (3.5)	.329	1406
Average Income Under $10,000						
(3)	-130	.118 (3.9)	-.0000013 (0.5)	—	.248	873
(4)	-106	.104 (3.4)	-.000005 (0.2)	14.9 (3.0)	.256	873
Less than $5,000						
(5)	-4	.061 (4.9)	—	13.6 (2.6)	.168	191
(6)	26	.084 (6.7)	—	14.6 (2.4)	.072	682
Average Income $10,000 or More						
(7)	274	.078 (5.5)	.000001 (3.6)	—	.100	533
(8)	214	.076 (5.4)	-.0000009 (3.5)	16.7 (1.7)	.105	533

NOTE: The figures shown in parentheses below the coefficients are t-ratios.

Table 6-3

DEMOGRAPHIC CORRELATES OF THE INDEX OF PAST AND EXPECTED FINANCIAL PROGRESS
(Percentage Distribution)

Demographic Characteristic	Index of Financial Progress					
	Pessimistic	0	1 to 3	4 and 5	Optimistic	Total
Average Annual Income						
Under $5,000	32	18	28	17	5	100
$5,000-7,499	10	16	38	22	14	100
$7,500-9,999	14	9	36	22	19	100
$10,000-14,999	12	9	34	20	25	100
$15,000 or more	8	7	33	22	30	100
Age of Head						
Under 30	6	6	27	30	31	100
30-39	9	11	31	26	23	100
40-49	18	13	40	17	12	100
50-59	23	15	38	14	10	100
Marital Status						
Married all years	13	11	35	21	20	100
Single all years	24	19	30	17	10	100
Single to married	9	7	37	20	27	100
Married to single	24	10	33	21	12	100
More than one change	9	14	45	27	5	100
Stage in Family Life Cycle						
Young, single	7	8	34	23	28	100
Young, married no children	9	7	28	31	25	100
Young, married, youngest child under 6	7	11	30	27	25	100
Young, married, youngest child 6 or older	12	8	38	19	23	100
Older, married, children at home	22	13	35	18	12	100
Older, married, no children at home	17	12	45	14	12	100
Older, single	28	24	32	12	4	100
Any age, single with children	22	15	31	19	13	100
Housing Status						
Owner						
Nonmover	16	13	37	17	17	100
Mover	7	8	35	27	23	100
Renter						
Nonmover	13	14	36	20	17	100
Mover	13	2	35	27	23	100
Change in housing status	16	12	25	27	20	100
All Families	14	12	35	21	18	100

NOTE: Age of head and stage in family life cycle are at the time of the
first interview. Young families are those whose head was under 45
at the time of the interview and older families are those whose
head was 45 years old or older.

Changes in life cycle status are also important, especially changes in marital status. The most significant differences here are for the group of panel members whose marital status changed from single to married during the course of the panel. These families were, on the whole, much more optimistic than other panel families. The other significant group is composed of those who either got divorced, separated, or became widowed during the panel. Not surprisingly these families frequently said that their financial position had worsened over the past year and they expected either no improvement or further deterioration over the coming year.

Given the pattern of correlations shown in Table 6-3, it is possible that part or even all of the observed influence of families' subjective evaluations of their financial progress is a spurious correlation, reflecting not the attitudes *per se* but other characteristics of the family unit. To examine the impact of the index net of the effects of other variables on expenditures, we ran a set of dummy variable regressions of the type described in detail in Chapter 4. The regression analysis of average annual expenditures on major durables included as predictors, in addition to the index of financial progress, average annual income, stage in the family life cycle, and major changes in life cycle stage over the course of the panel. The full range of the index was not used in the regressions. Rather it was collapsed into only seven categories ranging from highly pessimistic, which included families with scores of -3 or lower, to highly optimistic, which included families who reported always being better off and expecting to be still better off next year. The analysis was run for all families, and separately for families with an average annual income of less than $10,000 and for families with an income of $10,000 or more.

The adjusted deviations of expenditures on major durables from mean expenditure for the seven categories of the index are plotted in Graph 6-2 for each of the three regression analyses. As shown in the detailed analysis which is presented in Appendix Table 6-2 to this chapter, taking family characteristics other than income into account does reduce somewhat the magnitude of the influence on expenditures of attitudes toward financial progress in the regression for all families. Before adjustment the deviations range from -$269 to $447, while the deviations adjusted for income and differences in family life cycle range from -$119 to $210. However, as shown in the graph, expenditures on consumer durables are still strongly influenced by how people perceive their financial progress, and the general pattern of responses is unchanged. Again, the most striking difference is between families who are in the modal group—the moderately optimistic families—and families who consistently felt that their situation was improving. The families feeling consistent improvements spent on average 25 percent more on durables each year than did all families. As families mentioned more and more frequently that they were or thought that they could be worse off financially, expenditures gradually fell below the mean.

Graph 6-2
DEVIATION FROM MEAN EXPENDITURES ON MAJOR DURABLES BY PAST AND EXPECTED FINANCIAL PROGRESS AFTER ADJUSTMENT FOR DIFFERENCES IN ECONOMIC AND DEMOGRAPHIC SITUATION

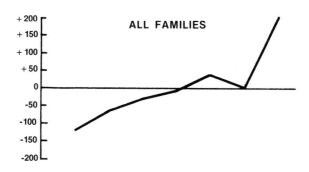

ALL FAMILIES

AVERAGE ANNUAL INCOME UNDER $10,000

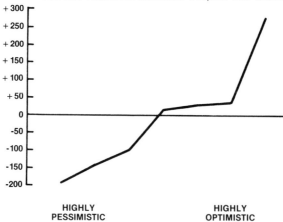

AVERAGE ANNUAL INCOME $10,000 OR MORE

HIGHLY   HIGHLY
PESSIMISTIC   OPTIMISTIC
index of financial progress

The separate analyses for families with average annual incomes of less than and greater than $10,000 are interesting because they modify somewhat the conclusions suggested by the regression in Table 6-2, which constrained the impact of attitudes to be linear and did not take into account factors other than income. For the lower of the two income groups, including family life cycle and major changes in life cycle in the analysis substantially reduces the amount by which pessimistic and optimistic families differ in their spending on consumer durables. The strong influence of pessimistic attitudes on expenditures, suggested by the unadjusted deviations, in particular, is reduced by including other family characteristics in the analysis.

In contrast to families with incomes under $10,000, where controlling for differences in other family characteristics reduces the impact of attitudes on expenditures, for families with incomes of $10,000 or more a year, taking account of other characteristics increases both the slope and the regularity of the impact of attitudes on investments in consumer durables. Here again the most striking change in the relation is for families with pessimistic attitudes. Here, however, the change is in the direction of increasing the negative impact on expenditures for those families who feel highly negative about their financial progress. For families with highly pessimistic outlooks, mean expenditures were only $29 below average before adjustment for differences in family situation, but were $191 below the average after accounting for differences in family situation.

Further study would no doubt add to our knowledge of how attitudes affect expenditures on major durables. However, the above analysis seems sufficient to make clear one important point: while income trends, as calculated in Chapter 5, do not lead to major differences in expenditures on major durables, perceptions by families of changes in their personal financial situation do. In addition, there is little evidence that the strength of the relation between expenditures and personal evaluations of changes in financial well being is largely the result of a spurious correlation between attitudes and demographic characteristics which are themselves important determinants of expenditure levels.

Subjective Financial Progress and Installment Debt

Satisfaction with past financial developments and the expectation of future progress have an even stronger influence on the use of installment debt than on purchases of consumer durables. As shown in Table 6-4, the ratio of installment debt to income increases steadily with the extent of optimism regarding changes in financial position. While for the panel as a whole installment debt balances averaged about 10 percent of family income, for families with highly pessimistic evaluations of changes in their financial situation, average installment debt balances barely exceeded 5 percent of annual income. In contrast, highly optimistic families maintained installment debt balances

Table 6-4

FOUR-YEAR RATIO OF OUTSTANDING INSTALLMENT DEBT TO INCOME
BY INDEX OF PAST AND EXPECTED FINANCIAL PROGRESS

(Class Means)[1]

Index of Financial Progress	All Families		Average Income Under $10,000		Average Income $10,000 or More	
	Mean	Number of Families	Mean	Number of Families	Mean	Number of Families
Highly pessimistic	5.4	58	6.2	45	2.7	13
(-1 to -4)	7.6	146	7.9	104	6.9	42
(0)	8.1	166	7.9	120	8.4	46
(1 to 3)	10.1	484	10.4	303	9.7	181
(4 to 5)	11.1	295	13.2	182	7.8	113
(6 to 7)	12.2	197	13.9	93	10.6	104
Highly optimistic	13.1	63	18.2	27	9.2	36
All Families	10.0	1409	10.7	874	8.9	535

[1] Mean ratios of outstanding installment debt to income are in percent.

equal to about 13 percent of their annual income.

The impact of subjective evaluations of progress are especially striking among families with average annual incomes below $10,000. Highly optimistic families here maintained installment debt balances three times greater in relation to their income than families with clearly pessimistic outlooks, and 80 percent higher than all families with an average income below $10,000.

In Graph 6-3 the mean ratios of installment debt balances to income are

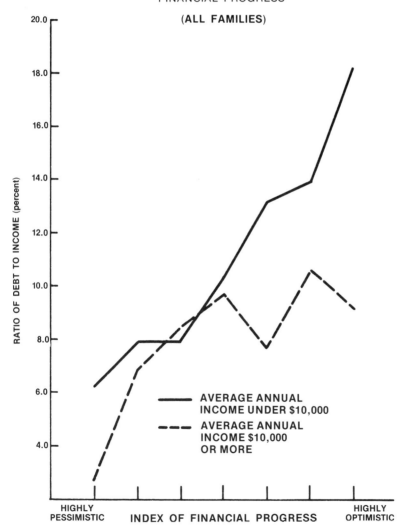

Graph 6-3
MEAN FOUR-YEAR RATIO OF OUTSTANDING INSTALLMENT
DEBT TO INCOME BY PAST AND EXPECTED
FINANCIAL PROGRESS

(ALL FAMILIES)

RATIO OF DEBT TO INCOME (percent)

—— AVERAGE ANNUAL
INCOME UNDER $10,000

- - - AVERAGE ANNUAL
INCOME $10,000
OR MORE

HIGHLY
PESSIMISTIC   INDEX OF FINANCIAL PROGRESS   HIGHLY
OPTIMISTIC

plotted separately for families with incomes of under and over $10,000 a year. For those with an income under $10,000 a year, not only do families with extreme attitudes differ dramatically, but installment debt balances are influenced by attitudes extending throughout the entire middle range of the index. Unlike with expenditures, even small differences in attitudes toward financial progress lead to different levels of installment debt use. Moderately pessimistic families, for example, maintained average balances relative to their income that were only about two-thirds as large as those maintained by families whose outlook was moderately optimistic, and both groups had ratios that differed substantially from the average ratio of installment debt to income maintained by all families with incomes of under $10,000.

The relation between felt financial progress and installment debt use is somewhat weaker for families who had an average annual income of $10,000 or more. Moreover, the relation is also asymmetric. Differences in average balances relative to income, between families who feel moderately optimistic about their financial outlook and families who are highly optimistic, are almost nonexistent among the higher income families in the panel. The most optimistic high income families in the panel, in fact, maintained lower balances than families who were slightly less optimistic, and differed almost not at all from families who reported most of the time that there had been no change in how well off they were financially and that they expected no change in the near future.

While optimism among higher income families did not appear to greatly influence installment debt use, higher income families who reported several times that they were worse off, or expected to be worse off by the end of next year, appear to have been strongly influenced by their pessimistic attitudes. Although the number of extremely pessimistic families was small, including only 13 of the 535 panel families with an average income of $10,000 or more, these families maintained almost no outstanding installment debt balances, less than 3 percent of their income, compared to an average of 8.9 percent for all higher income families.

In Table 6-5 responses of installment debt balances to differences in evaluations and expectations regarding financial progress are summarized in a set of regression equations which constrain the impact of attitudes to be linear. The regressions show that the impact of attitudes on dollar amounts of installment debt balances is three to four times as great as the impact of evaluations of financial progress on expenditures on major durables. Although the range of the index is fairly small, Table 6-5 indicates that each point on the index leads to a change in average installment debt balances of more than $50. Moreover, all of the coefficients on attitudes are about three times as large as their standard errors, and the addition of perceptions of past and expected progress increases the proportion of variance in installment debt balances explained by the regressions. The increase in explained variance is ex-

Table 6-5

REGRESSIONS OF AVERAGE OUTSTANDING INSTALLMENT DEBT ON INDEX OF PAST
AND EXPECTED FINANCIAL PROGRESS AND AVERAGE ANNUAL INCOME

| Income Group | Regression Coefficients | | | R^2 | Number of Families |
	Constant Term	Average Annual Income	Index of Financial Progress		
Average Income under $10,000 (1)	-217	.148 (13.5)	–	.172	874
(2)	-221	.131 (11.8)	53.1 (6.1)	.206	874
Less then $5,000 (3)	-70	.087 (4.4)	23.1 (2.8)	.151	197
$5,000-9,999 (4)	-228	.130 (5.8)	61.4 (5.6)	.093	677
Average Income $10,000 or More (5)	1200	-.0012 (0.1)	–	.000	535
(6)	990	–	58.7 (3.1)	.018	535

NOTE: The figures shown in parentheses below the coefficients are t-ratios.

pected, both because of the magnitude of the impact of the index and because that impact is distributed across the entire range of the index rather
than reflecting primarily differences between families at the extremes of the
index.

In terms of ratios of income to installment debt, both families with an income of under $5,000 and those with incomes ranging from $5,000 to $10,000
show similar responses (Table 6-6). For these families each point on the index
leads to an average change in installment debt balances of about six-tenths
of a percent of income. For families with an average income of $10,000 or
more, the estimated change is about four-tenths of a percentage point for
each change of one point on the index.

It is reassuring to find in regression (4) of Table 6-6 that the index of past
and expected financial progress is both statistically significant and has a
slope coefficient that is not neglible. As shown in Chapter 2, there is a strong
negative correlation between installment debt balances as a proportion of income and average annual income, for families with an income of $10,000 or
more a year. This negative correlation introduces an element of randomness
into tabulations, such as those in column (3) of Table 6-4, using debt to income ratios. Controlling for the random variation directly, by including income as well as the index of financial progress in regression (5) of Table 6-6,
indicates that the influence of the index on the extent of debt use shown in
Table 6-4 is not largely the result of how high income families are arrayed by
income within the various categories of the index of financial progress.

As in the case of expenditures on major durables, the influence of perception of financial progress has been re-evaluated using dummy variable regression techniques and including family life cycle and changes in life cycle
as well as average annual income and the index of financial progress. The adjusted deviations of installment debt from mean debt for each of the categories of the index are plotted for all families, families with an annual income
under $10,000 and higher income families in Graph 6-4.

Adjusting for differences in family life cycle does lead to reductions in the
deviations from average installment debt balances for most categories of the
index financial progress, especially at the extremes of the index. However, despite the strong correlation of family life cycle and debt use shown in Chapter
4, differences in perceptions of financial progress still lead to installment
debt balances that deviate from average balances for all families by several
hundred dollars. The differences in responses that were noted between families with incomes of over and under $10,000 persist even after adjustment for
differences in demographic situation. Indeed, controlling for other things
seems hardly to affect the pattern of responses by high income families to felt
financial progress. As shown in the detailed presentation of the dummy variable regressions in Appendix Table 6-3, including family life cycle in the
analysis led to only very minor adjustments in the responses of higher income
families to their own feelings about their financial progress.

Table 6-6

REGRESSIONS OF FOUR-YEAR RATIO OF OUTSTANDING INSTALLMENT DEBT TO INCOME
ON INDEX OF PAST AND EXPECTED FINANCIAL PROGRESS AND AVERAGE ANNUAL INCOME

Income Group	Regression Coefficients			R^2	Number of Families
	Constant Term	Average Annual Income	Index of Financial Progress		
Average Income under $10,000 (1)	4.3	.0007 (4.6)	.79 (6.5)	.087	874
Less than $5,000 (2)	2.2	.001 (2.2)	.62 (2.7)	.070	197
$5,000–9,999 (3)	9.4	.0007 (0.2)	.79 (5.6)	.045	677
Average Income $10,000 or More (4)	12.6	-.0003 (5.3)	.38 (2.7)	.059	535

NOTE: The figures shown in parentheses below the coefficients are t-ratios. The ratio of outstanding installment debt to income is a percent.

Graph 6-4
DEVIATION FROM MEAN OUSTANDING INSTALLMENT DEBT BY
PAST AND EXPECTED FINANCIAL PROGRESS AFTER
ADJUSTMENT FOR DIFFERENCES IN ECONOMIC AND
DEMOGRAPHIC SITUATION

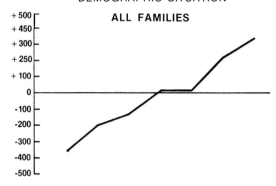

ALL FAMILIES

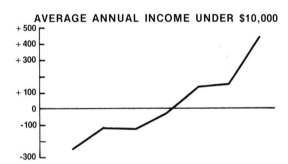

AVERAGE ANNUAL INCOME UNDER $10,000

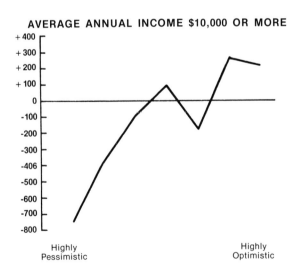

AVERAGE ANNUAL INCOME $10,000 OR MORE

Appendix Table 6-1

THE RELATION OF THE INDEX OF PAST AND EXPECTED FINANCIAL PROGRESS
AND THE RATE OF INCOME CHANGE
(Cell Means and Standard Deviations)

Index of Financial Progress	All Families		Average Income Under $10,000		Average Income $10,000 or More	
	Mean	Standard Deviation	Mean	Standard Deviation	Mean	Standard Deviation
Highly pessimistic	0.5	18.2	1.4	16.2	-2.8	24.5
(-1 to -2)	3.9	15.1	3.6	15.3	4.5	14.5
(0)	4.2	14.7	4.6	15.6	3.1	12.3
(1 to 3)	7.5	14.1	7.8	15.4	7.0	11.7
(4 to 5)	10.1	17.8	10.0	13.9	10.2	22.9
(6 to 7)	10.6	14.4	11.6	18.0	9.8	10.3
Highly optimistic	10.7	11.7	9.2	9.4	11.7	13.1
All Families	7.6	15.6	7.4	15.7	7.8	15.7

NOTE: The rate of income change is in percent per year. The cell
frequencies are similar to those in Table 6-3.

Appendix Table 6-2

RELATION OF PAST AND EXPECTED FINANCIAL PROGRESS TO EXPENDITURES
ON MAJOR DURABLES BEFORE AND AFTER ADJUSTMENT FOR DIFFERENCES
IN ECONOMIC AND DEMOGRAPHIC SITUATION

ALL PANEL FAMILIES

Predictors	Number of Families	Unadjusted Deviations	Adjusted Deviations
Average Annual Income (B^2=.281)			
Under $3,000	81	−691	−593
$3,000-4,999	110	−545	−479
$5,000-5,999	110	−312	−301
$6,000-7,499	195	−155	−145
$7,500-8,499	166	−77	−88
$8,500-9,999	211	18	3
$10,000-12,499	250	178	166
$12,500-14,999	133	365	331
$15,000-19,999	87	427	391
$20,000 or more	63	941	897
Index of Financial Progress (B^2=.009)			
Highly pessimistic	59	−269	−119
(−1 to −2)	143	−201	−64
(0)	164	−140	−30
(1 to 3)	490	−6	−8
(4 to 5)	291	70	39
(6 to 7)	198	116	4
Highly optimistic	61	447	210
Stage in Family Life Cycle (B^2=.012)			
Young, single	58	−151	−133
Young, married, no children	84	155	133
Young, married, youngest child under 6	412	11	4
Young, married, youngest child 6 or older	208	123	39
Older, married, children at home	266	111	41
Older, married, no children at home	212	11	−5
Older, single	82	−452	−150
Any age, single, with children	84	−349	−129
Major Change in Life Cycle (B^2=.007)			
Got married	48	−1	247
Became single	54	−202	−83
Last child left home	71	205	65
No children to having children	44	102	−43
More than one change in marital status	21	157	115
No major change	1168	−10	−11

NOTE: The dependent variable is four-year average annual expenditures on
major durables. The mean of the dependent variable is $811 (constant
term); the R^2 for the regression is .345. Unadjusted deviations are
univariate subgroup means expressed as deviations from the sample mean
of $811. The adjusted deviations are dummy variable regression co-
efficients under the constraint that the weighted sum of the set of
coefficients for a predictor equals zero. This yields the sample mean
of the dependent variable as the constant term of the regression.
There were 1406 families in the regression analysis.

Appendix Table 6-2 (con't)

FAMILIES WITH AVERAGE ANNUAL INCOMES OF LESS THAN $10,000

Predictors	Number of Families	Unadjusted Deviations	Adjusted Deviations
Average Annual Income (B^2=.192)			
Under $3,000	81	-474	-412
$3,000-4,999	110	-328	-284
$5,000-5,999	110	-94	-98
$6,000-7,499	195	62	55
$7,500-8,499	166	140	119
$8,500-9,999	211	235	212
Index of Fainancial Progress (B^2=.008)			
Highly pessimistic	46	-220	-84
(-1 to -2)	102	-136	-37
(0)	118	-66	11
(1 to 3)	309	-4	-24
(4 to 5)	179	81	45
(6 to 7)	94	130	34
Highly optimistic	25	239	107
Stage in Family Life Cycle (B^2=.017)			
Young, single	46	36	-29
Young, married, no children	54	218	129
Young, married, youngest child under 6	271	68	25
Young, married, youngest child 6 or older	111	132	53
Older, married, children at home	134	-35	-39
Older, married, no children at home	111	-55	14
Older, single	74	-267	-88
Any age, single, with children	72	-224	-113
Major Change in Life Cycle (B^2=.014)			
Got married	39	125	195
Became single	43	-135	-77
Last child left home	33	66	100
No children to having children	32	255	39
More than one change in marital status	13	132	150
No major change	713	-16	-15

NOTE: Mean expenditures = $594 (constant term); the R^2 for the regression
        is .262. There were 873 families in the regression analysis.

Appendix Table 6-2   (con't)

FAMILIES WITH AVERAGE ANNUAL INCOMES OF $10,000 OR MORE

Predictors	Number of Families	Unadjusted Deviations	Adjusted Deviations
Average Annual Income (B^2=.103)			
$10,000-12,499	250	-178	-149
$12,500-14,999	133	10	-97
$15,000-19,999	87	71	32
$20,000 or more	63	586	569
Index of Financial Progress (B^2=.019)			
Highly pessimistic	13	-29	-191
(-1 to -2)	41	-193	-142
(0)	46	-129	-99
(1 to 3)	181	6	17
(4 to 5)	112	45	31
(6 to 7)	104	-56	36
Highly optimistic	36	386	280
Stage in Family Life Cycle (B^2=.035)			
Young, single	12	-392	-493
Young, married, no children	30	76	144
Young, married, youngest child under 6	141	-37	-32
Young, married, youngest child 6 or older	97	6	22
Older, married, children at home	132	124	110
Older, married, no children at home	101	-33	-37
Older, single	8	-516	-636
Any age, single, with children	12	-151	-138
Major Change in Life Cycle (B^2=.012)			
Got married	9	36	472
Became single	11	29	-49
Last child left home	38	159	41
No children to having children	12	-83	-275
More than one change in marital status	8	193	95
No major change	455	-16	-6

NOTE: Mean expenditures = $1167 (constant term); the R^2 for the regression
is .132. There were 533 families in the regression analysis.

Appendix Table 6-3

RELATION OF PAST AND EXPECTED FINANCIAL PROGRESS TO AVERAGE INSTALLMENT
DEBT BALANCES BEGORE AND AFTER ADJUSTMENT FOR DIFFERENCES
IN ECONOMIC AND DEMOGRAPHIC SITUATION

ALL PANEL FAMILIES

Predictors	Number of Families	Unadjusted Deviations	Adjusted Deviations
Average Annual Income (B^2=.072)			
Under $3,000	83	-824	-643
$3,000-4,999	114	-595	-472
$5,000-5,999	111	-264	-246
$6,000-7,499	194	-127	-121
$7,500-8,499	165	40	11
$8,500-9,999	207	216	180
$10,000-12,499	253	306	274
$12,500-14,999	133	324	294
$15,000-19,999	86	215	159
$20,000 or more	63	-6	-51
Index of Financial Progress (B^2=.022)			
Highly pessimistic	58	-540	-373
(-1 to -2)	146	-316	-199
(0)	166	-243	-135
(1 to 3)	484	9	12
(4 to 5)	295	50	12
(6 to 7)	197	341	217
Highly optimistic	63	498	333
Stage in Family Life Cycle (B^2=.015)			
Young, single	63	-127	-216
Young, married, no children	85	212	159
Young, married, youngest child under 6	409	138	100
Young, married, youngest child 6 or older	207	197	81
Older, married, children at home	267	27	9
Older, married, no children at home	210	-240	-200
Older, single	84	-572	-194
Any age, single, with children	84	-193	-19
Major Change in Life Cycle (B^2=.005)			
Got married	54	178	350
Became single	57	-198	-10
Last child left home	70	176	101
No children to having children	44	182	-49
More than one change in marital status	21	46	106
No major change	1163	-17	-22

NOTE: The dependent variable is four-year average outstanding installment
debt. The mean of the dependent variable = $923 (constant term); the
R^2 for the regression is .130. Unadjusted deviations are univariate
subgroup means expressed as deviations from the sample mean of $923.
The adjusted deviations are dummy variable regression coefficients
under the constraint that the weighted sum of the set of coefficients
for a predictor equals zero. This yields the sample mean of the
dependent variable as the constant term of the regression. There
were 1409 families in the regression analysis.

Appendix Table 6-3 (con't)

FAMILIES WITH ANNUAL INCOMES OF LESS THAN $10,000

Predictors	Number of Families	Unadjusted Deviations	Adjusted Deviations
Average Annual Income (B^2=.114)			
Under $3,000	83	-665	-538
$3,000-4,999	114	-436	-353
$5,000-5,999	111	-106	-89
$6,000-7,499	194	31	20
$7,500-8,499	165	199	147
$8,500-9,999	207	376	323
Index of Financial Progress (B^2=.030)			
Highly pessimistic	45	-393	-256
(-1 to -2)	104	-253	-116
(0)	120	-234	-125
(1 to 3)	303	-17	-37
(4 to 5)	182	184	132
(6 to 7)	93	278	150
Highly optimistic	27	661	440
Stage in Family Life Cycle (B^2=.027)			
Young, single	51	10	-146
Young, married, no children	54	223	214
Young, married, youngest child under 6	267	170	96
Young, married, youngest child 6 or older	110	274	143
Older, married, children at home	134	-81	-80
Older, married, no children at home	110	-311	-205
Older, single	76	-426	-130
Any age, single, with children	72	-148	-31
Major Changes in Life Cycle (B^2=.017)			
Got married	45	283	359
Became single	46	9	121
Last child left home	31	105	173
No children to having children	32	148	-208
More than one change in marital status	13	-7	-236
No major change	707	-30	-28

NOTE: Mean outstanding installment debt = $764 (constant term); the R^2 for the regression was .218. There were 874 families in the regression analysis.

Appendix Table 6-3 (con't)

FAMILIES WITH ANNUAL INCOMES OF $10,000 OR MORE

Predictors	Number of Families	Unadjusted Deviations	Adjusted Deviations
Average Annual Income (B^2=.006)			
$10,000-12,499	253	47	44
$12,500-14,999	133	65	64
$15,000-19,999	86	-45	-48
$20,000 or more	63	-265	-248
Index of Financial Progress (B^2=.031)			
Highly pessimistic	13	-758	-752
(-1 to -2)	42	-337	-380
(0)	46	-114	-93
(1 to 3)	181	60	89
(4 to 5)	113	-169	-179
(6 to 7)	104	279	257
Highly optimistic	36	235	208
Stage in Family Life Cycle (B^2=.017)			
Young, single	12	-293	-478
Young, married, no children	31	209	141
Young, married, youngest child under 6	142	117	92
Young, married, youngest child 6 or older	97	31	34
Older, married, children at home	133	37	85
Older, married, no children at home	100	-246	-219
Older, single	8	-713	-771
Any age, single, with children	12	233	143
Major Change in Life Cycle (B^2=.007)			
Got married	9	182	290
Became single	11	-660	-530
Last child left home	39	100	53
No children to having children	12	438	301
More than one change in marital status	8	130	300
No major change	456	-10	-11

NOTE: Mean outstanding installment debt = $1182 (constant term); the R^2 for the regression is .022. There were 535 families in the regression analysis.

Chapter 7

ATTITUDES TOWARD INSTALLMENT DEBT

In Chapter 2 we examined the relation of average installment debt balances among income groups and noted the persistent upward shift in this function over the postwar period. Many factors have contributed to the shift. As noted by others, there have been substantial changes on the supply side of the consumer installment credit market. Maturities on installment loans have been lengthened and standards of credit-worthiness have been liberalized. Factors on the demand side of the market also have occurred, however, and one of the most important of these changes may well be in the attitudes which the American people hold toward the use of installment debt.

While the Survey Research Center has monitored attitudes toward installment credit for many years, the actual relationship between attitudes toward buying on the installment plan and the average amount of installment credit people use has not been extensively studied. In this chapter we examine the relationship between attitudes toward and the use of installment debt; relate changes in attitudes to credit use by the panel families; and examine changes in attitudes toward credit use over the 1960's using national cross-sectional data.

Measure of Attitudes

In order to measure people's attitudes toward installment buying, several approaches used by the Survey Research Center in the past were repeated in the first wave of the panel study. The questions were asked again in the fourth wave and, as will be shown later, a remarkable stability of the attitudes was reflected.

The question most often used by the Survey Research Center to ascertain people's attitudes toward installment debt has been: "Do you think it is a good idea or a bad idea for people to buy things on the installment plan?"

This question permits distinguishing answers which fall into the following categories: debt is a good idea, debt is a good idea qualified, debt has both good and bad aspects, debt is bad qualified, and debt is a bad idea.

Although this question was used often and is one of the few debt attitude questions on which good trend data exist, (as shown in Table 7-1) it does not discriminate well between high and low uses of installment debt. Only those who said that debt was unequivocably a good thing differ in the average level of outstanding installment debt maintained over the four-year period. Moreover, the differences among the other groups in Table 7-1 do not follow an easily explainable pattern.

A second approach proved more fruitful. Respondents were asked the following series of questions:

People have many different reasons for borrowing money which they pay back over a period of time. Would you say that it is all right for someone like yourself to borrow money...

    a) to cover expenses due to illness
    b) to cover the expenses of a vacation trip
    c) to finance the purchase of a fur coat or jewelry
    d) to cover living expenses when income is cut
    e) to finance educational expenses
    f) to finance the purchase of a car
    g) to finance the purchase of furniture
    h) to pay bills which have piled up

The proportion of respondents who felt it was legitimate to borrow for each of the above listed reasons varied greatly as indicated by the table below:

Appropriate to Borrow:	Proportion Responding "Yes"
To finance educational expenses	86
To cover expenses due to illness	85
To finance the purchase of a car	76
To finance the purchase of furniture	61
To pay bills which have piled up	49
To cover living expenses when income is cut	43
To cover the expenses of a vacation trip	10
To finance the purchase of a fur coat or jewelry	4

Moreover, the responses to these questions closely approximate a Guttman scale. If a respondent approves borrowing for the least frequently approved item, a fur coat or jewelry, he is likely also to approve borrowing to pay vacation expenses and all other purposes listed. If a respondent does not approve borrowing for a fur coat or jewelry, but does approve borrowing to cover va-

Table 7-1

AVERAGE OUTSTANDING INSTALLMENT DEBT BY GENERAL FEELING
TOWARD THE USE OF INSTALLMENT CREDIT
(Class Means)

Installment Buying is:	Average Income under $10,000		Average Income $10,000 or more	
	Four-year average debt, $	Ratio of debt to income	Four-year average debt, $	Ratio of debt to income
Good idea	890	12.6	1360	10.6
Good idea, qualified	745	9.7	1150	8.9
Pro-con	740	10.8	1100	7.2
Bad idea, qualified	850	11.0	835	6.5
Bad idea	620	8.9	1090	8.1
All Families	764	10.7	1182	8.9

cation expenses, he is likely to approve borrowing for all or almost all of the more frequently approved purposes. In all instances except two, two-thirds or more of the respondents who approved borrowing for one item on the list also agreed that it was all right to borrow for the next most frequently approved item. These findings reflect the relative agreement among Americans about the legitimacy of borrowing for different purposes, and when combined into an index where each "yes" response is given a weight of +1 point, and each "no" response a weight of zero, the index is a good indicator of how favorably disposed a person is toward the use of installment credit.[1]

The distribution of the index, which ranges from zero for respondents who did not feel it was legitimate to borrow money for any of the purposes listed to 8 for respondents who thought it was all right to borrow for all purposes listed, was as follows:[2]

Number of "yes" Responses	Proportion of Families
0	2
1	4
2	9
3	16
4	26
5	22
6	17
7	3
8	1
All Families	100

Attitudes and Installment Debt Balances

Since the debt attitude index defined above seems to capture fairly well attitudes toward buying on credit, it is not surprising to find that attitudes are associated with striking differences in amounts borrowed. As shown in Table

---

[1] Several attempts to combine the more general and more specific measures of attitudes toward installment debt use did not prove fruitful. One attempt to adjust the simple index described above by whether the respondent felt buying on the installment plan was in general a good or bad idea did seem promising, but the interaction of the two variables was not straightforward and the marginal gain in explaining debt levels did not seem worth the added complexity.

[2] The use of the index for the purpose of explaining borrowing may appear to be somewhat tautological. Asking someone whether it is all right to buy a car on the installment plan seems quite similar to asking whether he buys cars on the installment plan. It should be noted, however, that the index makes use of answers to eight questions, rather than one, and is used to predict not just whether a family will borrow, but also how much it will borrow. Thus, the answers are seen to reflect attitudes toward using debt, rather than to indicate merely the kinds of purchases the family itself would finance by borrowing.

7-2, the ratio of outstanding installment debt to income for families with highly favorable attitudes is more than twice as high as that for those with very unfavorable attitudes. For example, for a family with an income of $8,000, the difference in the amount of average outstanding installment debt, implied by the data in Table 7-2, between having very unfavorable and very favorable attitudes toward debt, is almost $600. The average amount of outstanding installment debt for all families with an average income between $7,500 and $8,500 was $960.

Although attitudes strongly affect installment debt use, being favorably disposed toward buying on the installment plan does not usually lead to the incurrence of excessive amounts of debt. Among families who agreed that it was okay to borrow for all of the reasons listed in the questionnaire, even to purchase fur coats and jewelry, average outstanding installment debt balances were only 12.5 percent of average annual income or about one and a half month's income.

In studying both calculated income trends and people's feelings about changes in their financial situation, we found that the use of debt by higher income families was either less strongly affected or influenced in a less predictable way than was the behavior of families in the panel with an income of more than $10,000 a year. This is not the case for attitudes toward the use of installment credit, however. As shown in column (3) of Table 7-2, higher income families with very negative opinions of installment debt use maintained average balances equal to 4.4 percent of their annual incomes. In contrast, families who were favorably disposed toward debt use for about half of the purposes listed maintained balances, on average, of about 9 percent of their incomes, and families very favorably disposed maintained even higher balances on average. This pattern of responses is very much the same as that observed for families with an average annual income below $10,000 in column (2) of Table 7-2.

The importance of attitudes is further verified by the regressions in Table 7-3. Among higher income families—regression (4)—attitudes alone explain about 3 percent of the variance in installment debt balances. More interesting, each point on the index of debt attitudes is associated with a change of $140 in average outstanding balances. Thus, the regression implies that changes in attitudes toward debt use by large numbers of families with relatively high incomes could greatly increase or decrease the total demand for consumer installment credit.

In Table 7-3, families with an income of less than $10,000 are divided into two groups, those with an income of less than $5,000 and those with an income of greater than $5,000, and separate regressions are shown for each group. Among families with an average income of between $5,000 and $10,000—about half of the panel families—attitudes are a highly significant predictor of installment debt use both statistically and in terms of the magni-

Table 7-2

FOUR-YEAR RATIO OF OUTSTANDING INSTALLMENT DEBT TO INCOME
BY ATTITUDE TOWARD INSTALLMENT DEBT USE
(Class Means)

Index of Attitude Toward Installment Debt	All Families	Average Income Under $10,000	Average Income $10,000 or More
Very unfavorable	5.3	5.6	4.4
(Score of 2)	7.8	9.4	4.8
(Score of 3)	9.2	9.5	8.6
(Score of 4)	9.8	10.4	8.8
(Score of 5)	11.0	11.7	9.9
(Score of 6)	12.4	13.6	10.4
Very favorable	12.5	12.9	12.2
All Families	10.0	10.7	8.9

Table 7-3

REGRESSIONS OF FOUR-YEAR AVERAGE OUTSTANDING INSTALLMENT DEBT
ON ATTITUDE TOWARD INSTALLMENT DEBT USE AND AVERAGE ANNUAL INCOME

| Income Group | Regression Coefficients | | | R^2 | Number of Families |
	Constant Term	Average Annual Income	Debt Attitude Index		
Average income under $10,000					
(1)	−217	.148 (13.5)	−	.172	874
(2)	−440	.141 (12.8)	66.3 (4.3)	.190	874
Less than $5,000					
(3)	−124	.096 (4.9)	12.3 (1.0)	.121	197
$5,000-9,999					
(4)	−492	.137 (6.0)	87.6 (4.4)	.076	˙677
Average income $10,000 or more					
(5)	570	−	143.6 (4.1)	.030	535

NOTE: The figures shown in parentheses below the coefficients are t-ratios.

tude of the impact. As shown in regression (4) of Table 7-3, a change of one point in the attitude index leads to a change in average outstanding installment debt balances of about $88 for these middle income families. For families in the panel with average incomes of less than $5,000, on the other hand, attitudes toward debt bear almost no relation to installment debt balances. The index is not a statistically significant predictor of debt balances, and the magnitude of the coefficient on attitudes, being only $12, is too small to consider important.

It is perhaps not surprising that attitudes bear little relation to debt use for lower income families. The ability to repay debt and confidence in the future stream of income are likely to override personal preferences here.

In Table 7-4, regressions are presented which summarize the influence of attitudes on outstanding installment debt balances as a proportion of income. The coefficients on the debt attitude index in these regressions make even clearer the potential importance of the role of changing attitudes in contributing to aggregate trends in the demand for consumer credit. For all panel families with an income of $5,000 a year or more, a change in the index of a single point—that is, feeling it is all right to borrow for one more or one fewer of the items included in the index—leads, on average, to a change in installment debt balances equal to 1 percent of income.[3]

Change in Attitudes Among Panel Families

The argument that change in attitudes toward installment buying over time will directly affect the demand for consumer installment credit would be strengthened if it could be shown that change in attitudes on the part of panel families lead to changes in the use of installment debt.

The questions on attitudes toward debt use, asked in the first year's interview, were repeated at the time of the last interview three years later. By having both beginning and end of period measures of attitudes toward debt use, we can get some notion of how stable attitudes are over several years, and can attempt to discern whether the changes we observe are real changes in attitudes or simply reflect the fact that some people are better respondents than others.

In Table 7-5 the scores on the index in the first year of the panel are compared with fourth year scores. Somewhat more than one-quarter of the scores were identical in both years. An additional 40 percent of the scores changed

---

[3]The coefficients on income in regressions (2) to (4) of Table 7-4 are indicative of the relation between income and use of installment debt discussed earlier (see Chapter 2). At low income levels increases in income are associated with increases in installment debt more than in proportion to the increase in income; middle income families ($5,000-$9,999) increase their installment debt balances in proportion to their income, and hence the coefficient on income in regression (3) is insignificant; and finally, at incomes of $10,000 or more, increases in income are associated with increases in installment debt less than in proportion to the change in income.

Table 7-4

REGRESSIONS OF FOUR-YEAR RATIO OF OUTSTANDING INSTALLMENT DEBT
TO INCOME ON ATTITUDE TOWARD INSTALLMENT DEBT USE AND AVERAGE
ANNUAL INCOME

Income Group	Regression Coefficients			R^2	Number of families
	Constant term	Average annual income	Debt attitude index		
Average income under $10,000					
(1)	11.2	.0008 (5.5)	.98 (4.6)	.064	874
Less than $5,000					
(2)	8.6	.0014 (2.6)	.30 (0.9)	.041	197
$5,000-9,999					
(3)	5.9	.0002 (0.5)	1.16 (4.4)	.029	677
Average income $10,000 or more					
(4)	8.8	-.0003 (4.8)	1.06 (4.1)	.075	535

NOTE: The figures shown in parentheses below the coefficients
are t-ratios. The ratio of outstanding installment debt
to income is a percent.

Table 7-5

ATTITUDE TOWARD INSTALLMENT DEBT USE IN EARLY 1967 BY ATTITUDE
THREE YEARS LATER FOR THE SAME FAMILIES
(Frequency Distribution)

Number of Favorable Responses in Early 1967	Number of Favorable Responses in Early 1970									Number of Families	Percent of Families
	None	One	Two	Three	Four	Five	Six	Seven	Eight		
None	5	5	4	7	6	2	4	–	–	33	2
One	9	5	15	5	9	8	–	–	–	51	4
Two	5	12	28	26	39	13	9	–	1	133	9
Three	5	19	33	57	53	39	17	3	1	227	16
Four	6	10	18	77	92	110	44	5	4	366	26
Five	4	8	13	33	65	89	77	10	3	302	22
Six	2	4	8	22	34	71	83	9	5	238	17
Seven	–	–	3	2	7	9	13	4	7	45	3
Eight	–	–	1	–	4	3	4	–	2	14	1
Number of Families	36	63	123	229	309	344	251	31	23	1409	
Percent of Families	3	4	9	16	22	24	18	2	2		100

by only a single point. For the remaining one-third of the families, the index values calculated on the basis of the final year's data differed from the initial year's index value by two points or more. About 14 percent of all respondents had differences of three points or more in the index. The changes in the index scores were neither overwhelmingly in the direction of more favorable attitudes toward debt use nor in the direction of less favorable attitudes. Yet, favorable changes in attitudes were slightly more frequent than changes in the direction of less favorable attitudes.

Unlike the attitudes discussed in Chapter 6, we expect that for very many families attitudes toward installment debt use will be stable over long periods of time and subject to revision only infrequently. The data in Table 7-6 verify these expectations. Two-thirds of the panel families had attitude scores that were within one point of each other when the measures of attitudes are separated by three full years. Moreover, the evidence of Table 7-5 shows convincingly that, whether or not changes in attitudes as measured by the index are meaningful, the index is a reliable measure of attitudes which could be used to monitor the general level of attitudes toward installment debt over time.

In Table 7-6 the ratio of installment debt to income has been calculated separately for families whose scores on the index of attitudes toward credit buying did not change by more than one point between the first and the fourth years of the panel. When only families with such stable attitudes are considered, the relation between debt use and attitudes toward it is even more striking than when all families are considered together, regardless of whether their attitudes had changed. The extent of the improvement in the relation is made even more dramatic in Graph 7-1 where average ratios of installment debt to income are plotted separately for families with stable attitudes and for all families.

While the data in Table 7-6 and the accompanying graph show that the impact of attitudes on debt use is even greater when families with stable measures of attitudes are considered separately, they do not tell us whether the changes in index scores represent meaningful changes in the disposition of families toward installment buying, or merely random measurement error. In order to test whether the changes in the index represent real changes of opinion, we reran the regressions presented in Table 7-2 including changes in attitudes as well as their initial level. The change variable used in the regressions was obtained by subtracting the value of the index in the fourth year of the panel from its value in the first year for each family.

As shown in Table 7-7, the variable change in attitudes has a statistically significant impact on debt use. The statistical significance of the change variable is noteworthy because some families may not have changed their attitudes until late in the panel study, and for families with changes in the direction of less favorable attitudes it might take some time until the level of out-

Table 7-6

FOUR-YEAR RATIO OF OUTSTANDING INSTALLMENT DEBT TO INCOME BY ATTITUDE
TOWARD INSTALLMENT DEBT USE FOR FAMILIES WITH STABLE ATTITUDES[1]
(Class Means)

Index of Attitude Toward Installment Debt	Average Income Under $10,000	Average Income $10,000 or More
Very unfavorable attitudes	5.3	1.4[a]
(Score of 2)	7.0	2.4
(Score of 3)	11.1	8.1
(Score of 4)	12.0	9.7
(Score of 5)	15.0	10.3
(Score of 6)	15.2	11.8
Very favorable attitudes	17.9[a]	15.6[a]
All Families	12.6	9.5

---

[1]Attitudes were considered stable if the index scores of the family for the first and fourth years of the panel differed by no more than one point.

[a]Cell contains twenty or fewer families.

Graph 7-1
MEAN FOUR-YEAR RATIO OF OUTSTANDING INSTALLMENT
DEBT TO INCOME BY ATTITUDE TOWARD INSTALLMENT DEBT
USE SHOWING ALL FAMILIES AND FAMILIES WITH
STABLE ATTITUDES

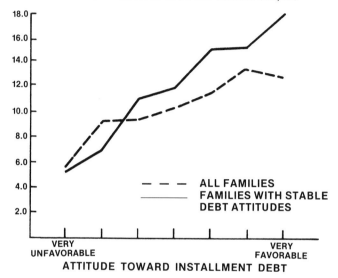

AVERAGE ANNUAL INCOME UNDER $10,000

ATTITUDE TOWARD INSTALLMENT DEBT

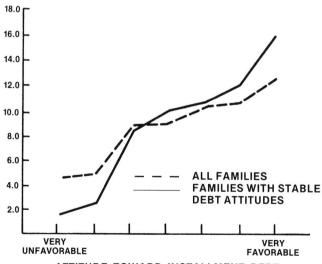

AVERAGE ANNUAL INCOME $10,000 OR MORE

ATTITUDE TOWARD INSTALLMENT DEBT

standing debt is actually reduced to the level appropriate to the changed attitudes.

We would expect that families who moved higher or lower on the attitude scale would, after the transition, behave on average as families who have held similar attitudes for quite some time. The smaller coefficient on attitude change probably reflects the fact that people whose attitudes changed may have made those changes either very soon after the first interview or very near the last interview.

Inclusion of changes in attitudes toward installment debt use, in addition to initial attitudes, increases appreciably the impact of attitudes on installment debt balances, and at the same time appreciably decreases the standard errors on the coefficients of initial attitudes. For example, when changes in attitudes are not included, the change in the debt-to-income ratio for families with an income of less than $10,000 associated with a difference of one point in the initial attitude index is .98—regression (1), Table 7-4. However, as shown in Table 7-7, when attitude change is also included, a difference of 1 point on the attitude index is associated with a change in installment debt of 1.5 percent of income.

Attitudes and Family Life Cycle

To arrive at a final assessment of the impact of attitudes on debt use, we take into account in this section not only income and attitude change, but also other characteristics of the family. As indicated by the data in Appendix Table 7-1 to this chapter, attitudes of families at different stages of the family life cycle differ considerably. About 50 percent of all families with children felt that it was all right to borrow for at least 5 of the 8 purposes included in the index. Only 37 percent of older couples with no children at home felt it was all right to borrow for as many as five of the purposes listed, however, and among older single people only 21 percent felt that five or more of the purposes listed were legitimate reasons to incur debt. Indeed, among older single people, 39 percent felt it was not all right to borrow for more than one of the reasons included in the index, while only 10 to 13 percent of families with children held such negative opinions of borrowing.

We sought to estimate the impact of attitudes toward installment debt "net" of family life cycle effects which were shown in Chapter 4 to influence the use of installment debt very strongly. To do this, a dummy variable regression was run which included average annual income, family life cycle, change in life cycle status, attitudes toward installment buying and changes in these attitudes between the first and fourth interviews of the panel, as predictors of average outstanding installment debt balances. The analysis was run for all families and then for families with average incomes of less than and more than $10,000, separately. The deviations of families more or less favorably disposed toward debt from the mean installment debt balances are

Table 7-7

REGRESSIONS OF FOUR-YEAR AVERAGE OUTSTANDING INSTALLMENT DEBT
AND DEBT TO INCOME RATIO ON CHANGE IN ATTITUDE TOWARD INSTALLMENT DEBT USE

	Regression Coefficients					
	Constant term	Average annual income	Debt attitude index	Change in debt attitude index	Age of head	R^2
Average income under $10,000						
Outstanding instalment debt						
(1)	-12	.129 (11.9)	84.7 (4.7)	46.5 (2.9)	-10.7 (5.0)	.223
Ratio of debt to income						
(2)	3.6	-	1.8 (7.0)	1.1 (4.6)	-	.054
(3)	12.0	-	1.5 (5.8)	.87 (3.8)	-.18 (6.1)	.093
Average income $10,000 or more						
Outstanding instalment debt						
(4)	1293	-	171.4 (4.3)	75.0 (2.0)	-19.8 (3.4)	.059
Ratio of debt to income						
(5)	7.3	-.0003 (4.8)	1.4 (4.7)	.65 (2.4)	-	.085
(6)	13.7	-.0003 (4.4)	1.3 (4.4)	.61 (2.2)	-.15 (3.4)	.104

NOTE: The figures shown in parentheses below the coefficients are t-ratios. The subheadings within income groups indicate the dependent variable used. The ratio of outstanding installment debt to income is a percent.

plotted in Graph 7-2. The detailed regression analyses are shown in Appendix Table 7-3.

Even after taking account of other factors which influence installment debt use, the impact of attitudes on outstanding balances is striking. In the analysis of all families, where deviations are, in effect, the weighted average of the deviations from the two income subgroup analyses, families with highly favorable or highly unfavorable attitudes have deviations from the average balance of the panel of over $300. This indicates that differences in attitudes alone lead to the maintenance of installment debt balances that are, on average, more than 30 percent higher or lower than the average for all families. Even panel families with less extreme attitudes maintained, on average, installment debt balances that deviated from the norm by $200 or more.

The most striking difference between the separate analyses for families with incomes of under and over $10,000 is in the slopes of the plotted relations in Graph 7-2. The deviations around the average balance maintained by the two subgroups are about the same in terms of percentages. Families with highly favorable or highly unfavorable attitudes had differences in average balances of about 40 percent of the mean of the subgroup in both cases. However, the differences for high income families in terms of dollar magnitudes were about $200 larger than those for families with highly favorable or highly unfavorable attitudes but with an average annual income of less than $10,000.

The great sensitivity of average installment debt balances among higher income families is undoubtedly partly the result of the great amount of discretion which these families have in how they choose to finance large purchases. Moreover, these data indicate that using installment debt is very often not associated with a need to borrow. Rather, the extent to which a family relies on credit as a means of finance may be largely a matter of personal preference.

The results of the regression analyses which take into account not only income but also other characteristics of the family further reinforce the assertion made earlier in this chapter that changes in attitudes toward buying on credit, especially changes among high income families, are likely to have a substantial impact on the demand for consumer credit. Furthermore, steady trends toward more favorable attitudes over time, coupled with the increased availability of consumer credit, could have accounted for a very substantial part of the shift in debt use among income groups over the postwar period.

Change in Attitudes over the 1960's

Throughout this chapter it has been shown that attitudes are important and that changes in them will lead to changes in the aggregate demand for consumer installment credit. However, the extent to which changes in attitudes have actually contributed to the postwar growth in installment debt depends, quite obviously, on the extent to which attitudes have in fact changed

Graph 7-2
DEVIATION FROM MEAN OUTSTANDING INSTALLMENT DEBT BY
ATTITUDE TOWARD INSTALLMENT DEBT USE AFTER
ADJUSTMENT FOR DIFFERENCES IN ECONOMIC AND
DEMOGRAPHIC SITUATION

ALL FAMILIES

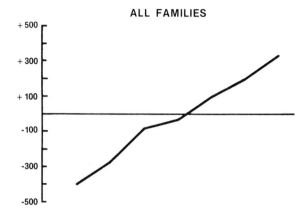

AVERAGE ANNUAL INCOME UNDER $10,000

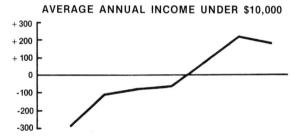

AVERAGE ANNUAL INCOME $10,000 OR MORE

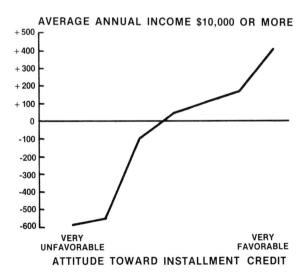

over the period. In this section we attempt to get some notion of the extent of attitude change at least over the 1960's, by using data from the archives of the Survey Research Center.

The sequence of questions from which the index of debt attitudes was constructed was asked by the Survey Research Center in 1959. In Table 7-8 the proportion of families who felt it was appropriate to borrow for each of the items included in the index is shown for all families as well as for families with incomes between $7,500 and $9,999 and families with an income of $10,000 or more. The 1967 incomes were converted into 1959 dollars so that the income ranges in Table 7-8 are comparable for the two years, 1959 and 1967.

It appears that attitudes toward credit use changed markedly over the seven-year period between late 1959 and early 1967. A few components of the index showed some decline. Generally, however, the direction of change was toward more favorable attitudes. The most striking change was in the proportion of respondents who felt that it was all right to borrow to cover living expenses when income declined. While only 26 percent of the people interviewed in 1959 felt borrowing to cover living expenses was appropriate for families like themselves, 40 percent of those interviewed in 1967 felt that borrowing under such circumstances was appropriate. The reasons for this change are not known. Possibly, after several good years in the 1960's the American people came to consider income declines more transitory than before, and therefore the proportion approving borrowing in cases of income declines increased.

Some other purposes of borrowing, toward which a larger proportion of families felt more favorably disposed in 1967 than in 1959, are for items which have in the past been considered primarily luxury goods. These are furniture, vacations, and fur coats and jewelry. The increase was greatest for purchases of furniture, where 8 percent more people felt this was an appropriate reason to incur debt in 1967 than had felt that way in 1959. Four percent more families felt it was all right for people like themselves to borrow to cover vacation expenses, and 2 percent more approved of borrowing to buy furs and jewelry.

Since middle and upper-middle income families account for a very substantial portion of installment debt use, and since these families are particularly strongly influenced by their attitudes toward debt, changes in their attitudes are of special interest. As shown in Table 7-8, the attitudes of families with middle-range incomes and above have become generally more favorable towards several items on the list. Among families with an income of $10,000 or more (in 1959 dollars), 19 percent more approved of borrowing to purchase a car in 1967 than in 1959, 18 percent more approved of borrowing to cover living expenses when income is cut, 17 percent more approved of borrowing to purchase furniture, 8 percent more approved vacation expenses, and 4 percent more felt it was appropriate to borrow to buy a fur coat or jewelry.

Table 7-8

TRENDS IN ATTITUDES TOWARD INSTALLMENT DEBT USE, 1959-1967

(Percentage Distribution)

Appropriate Purposes for Borrowing	All Families		Total Family Income			
			$7,500-9,999		$10,000 or more	
	1959	1967	1959	1967	1959	1967
To cover expenses due to illness	86	80	86	84	85	86
To finance educational expenses	70	77	81	82	83	88
To finance the purchase of a car	67	65	74	79	61	80
To finance the purchase of furniture	44	52	49	61	41	58
To pay bills which have piled up	44	43	39	43	40	40
To cover living expenses when income is cut	26	40	21	40	23	41
To cover the expenses of a vacation	5	9	8	10	5	13
To finance the purchase of a fur coat or jewelry	2	4	3	4	3	7

NOTE: Each cell is the proportion of all families interviewed who agreed that borrowing was appropriate for the specified purpose. Income is in 1959 dollars. Figures were obtained from national cross-section surveys of the Survey Research Center.

There can be little doubt that the attitudes of the American people toward buying on credit have become more favorable over the past decade. Moreover, although little is known about the origins of attitudes toward installment borrowing and the factors that cause these attitudes to change, it seems reasonable that changing attitudes have been very much related to the rapid growth of installment debt over the postwar period. Future rates of growth of installment debt will depend, of course, on many factors. However, trends in attitudes toward credit buying will be highly influential and deserve further study.

Appendix Table 7-1

DEMOGRAPHIC CORRELATES OF ATTITUDES TOWARD THE USE OF INSTALLMENT CREDIT
(Percentage Distribution)

Demographic Characteristic	Debt Attitude Index					
	Unfavorable Attitudes	Score of 3	Score of 4	Score of 5	Favorable Attitudes	Total
Average Annual Income						
Under $5,000	25	18	22	19	16	100
$5,000-7,499	15	16	25	21	23	100
$7,500-9,999	12	14	31	23	20	100
$10,000-14,999	12	16	25	22	25	100
$15,000 or more	16	19	26	21	18	100
Age of Head						
Under 30	9	17	26	23	25	100
30-39	14	18	23	23	22	100
40-49	15	14	29	22	20	100
50-59	22	16	26	18	18	100
Marital Status						
Married all years	13	15	27	22	23	100
Single all years	27	22	24	15	12	100
Single to married	18	11	16	28	27	100
Married to single	17	14	19	28	22	100
More than one change	14	36	23	14	14	100
Stage in Family Life Cycle						
Young, single	16	14	18	24	28	100
Young, married, no children	16	22	29	15	18	100
Young, married, youngest child under 6	10	16	27	22	25	100
Young, married, youngest child 6 or older	10	17	24	26	23	100
Older, married, children at home	13	13	27	23	24	100
Older, married, no children at home	21	13	29	18	19	100
Older, single	39	16	23	9	13	100
Any age, single with children	16	27	25	24	8	100
Housing Status						
Owner						
Nonmover	15	16	28	19	22	100
Mover	10	18	24	27	21	100
Renter						
Nonmover	20	15	21	22	22	100
Mover	16	17	27	26	14	100
Other, change in status	15	16	25	23	21	100
Education of Head						
Less than 12 grades	19	15	26	20	20	100
High school diploma	12	14	26	25	23	100
Some college, no degree	14	21	26	23	16	100
College degree	16	18	26	15	25	100
All Families	15	16	27	21	21	100

NOTE: Age of head, stage in family life cycle and education of head are at the time of the first interview. Young families are those whose head was under age 45 at the time of the interview. Older families are those whose head was age 45 or older.

Appendix Table 7-2

DEMOGRAPHIC CORRELATES OF CHANGE IN ATTITUDES
TOWARD THE USE OF INSTALLMENT CREDIT
(Percentage Distribution)

Demographic Characteristic[1]	Change in Debt Attitude Index[2]			
	Favorable Change	No Change	Unfavorable Change	Total
Average Annual Income				
Under $5,000	19	61	20	100
$5,000-7,499	18	66	16	100
$7,500-9,999	16	69	15	100
$10,000-14,999	17	68	15	100
$15,000 or more	17	68	15	100
Income Trend (percent per year)				
-10.0 percent or less	17	56	27	100
-5.0 to -9.9	17	65	18	100
0.0 to -4.9	12	69	19	100
0.1 to 4.9	14	69	17	100
5.0 to 9.9	20	68	12	100
10.0 to 14.9	19	67	14	100
15.0 to 19.9	9	69	23	100
20.0 percent or more	22	69	9	100
Stage in Family Life Cycle				
Young, single	18	71	11	100
Young, married, no children	18	65	17	100
Young, married, youngest child under 6	16	69	15	100
Young, married, youngest child 6 or older	17	67	16	100
Older, married, children at home	15	66	19	100
Older, married, no children at home	19	64	17	100
Older, single	20	68	12	100
Any age, single with children	21	63	16	100
Marital Status				
Married all years	17	67	16	100
Single all years	19	68	13	100
Single to married	21	67	12	100
Married to single	14	64	22	100
More than one change	23	63	14	100
All Families	18	66	16	100

---

[1] Stage in family life cycle at the time of the first interview. Young families are those whose head was under age 45 at the time of the interview. Older families are those whose head was age 45 or older.

[2] A change in attitudes is defined as a movement of 2 or more points on the debt attitude index between the time of the first interview in early 1967 and the last interview in early 1970.

Appendix Table 7-3

RELATION OF ATTITUDES TOWARD INSTALLMENT DEBT USE TO OUTSTANDING INSTALLMENT
DEBT BEFORE AND AFTER ADJUSTMENT FOR DIFFERENCE IN ECONOMIC
AND DEMOGRAPHIC SITUATION

ALL PANEL FAMILIES

Predictors	Number of Families	Unadjusted Deviations	Adjusted Deviations
Average Annual Income (B^2=.081)			
Under $3,000	83	−824	−675
$3,000-4,999	114	−595	−512
$5,000-5,999	111	−264	−264
$6,000-7,499	194	−127	−139
$7,500-8,499	165	40	5
$8,500-9,999	207	217	177
$10,000-12,499	253	306	278
$12,500-14,999	133	324	311
$15,000-19,999	86	215	210
$20,000 or more	63	−6	48
Debt Attitude Index (B^2=.029)			
Very unfavorable attitudes	84	−527	−398
(Score of 2)	133	−290	−276
(Score of 3)	227	−59	−80
(Score of 4)	366	−6	−26
(Score of 5)	302	114	101
(Score of 6)	238	178	201
Very favorable attitudes	59	371	336
Change in Debt Attitude Index (B^2=.008)			
Less favorably inclined	224	−61	−150
Somewhat favorably inclined	280	−39	−93
No change	365	90	65
Somewhat more favorably inclined	302	41	48
More favorably inclined	238	−87	90
Stage in Family Life Cycle (B^2=.016)			
Young, single	63	−127	−183
Young, married, no children	85	212	231
Young, married, youngest child under 6	409	13	108
Young, married, youngest child 6 or older	207	197	72
Older, married, children at home	267	27	1
Older, married, no children at home	210	−240	−200
Older, single	84	−572	−160
Any age, single, with children	84	−193	−45

Appendix Table 7- 3 (con't)

ALL PANEL FAMILIES

Predictors	Number of Families	Unadjusted Deviations	Adjusted Deviations
Major Change in Life Cycle (B^2=.005)			
Got married	54	178	355
Became single	57	-198	-8
Last child left home	70	176	89
No children to having children	44	182	-69
More than one change in marital status	21	45	86
No major change	1163	-17	-20

NOTE: The dependent variable is four-year average outstanding installment
        debt. The mean of the dependent variable = $923 (constant term);
        the R^2 for the regression is .132. Unadjusted deviations are
        univariate subgroup means expressed as deviations from the sample
        mean of $923. The adjusted deviations are dummy variable regression
        coefficients under the constraint that the weighted sum of the set
        of coefficients for a predictor equals zero. This yields the sample
        mean of the dependent variable as the constant term of the regression.
        There were 1409 families in the regression analysis.

Appendix Table 7-3 (con't)

FAMILIES WITH AVERAGE ANNUAL INCOMES OF LESS THAN $10,000

Predictors	Number of Families	Unadjusted Deviations	Adjusted Deviations
Average Annual Income (B^2=.127)			
Under $3,000	83	-665	-554
$3,000-4,999	114	-436	-378
$5,000-5,999	111	-106	-113
$6,000-7,499	194	31	22
$7,500-8,499	165	199	166
$8,500-9,999	207	376	338
Debt Attitude Index (B^2=.031)			
Very unfavorable attitudes	59	-434	-295
(Score of 2)	86	-114	-111
(Score of 3)	135	-91	-79
(Score of 4)	234	-26	-64
(Score of 5)	187	100	83
(Score of 6)	149	203	222
Very favorable attitudes	24	200	168
Change in Debt Attitude Index (B^2=.010)			
Less favorably inclined	145	-71	-132
Somewhat favorably inclined	173	5	-41
No change	224	34	10
Somewhat more favorably inclined	183	16	25
More favorably inclined	149	-6	130
Stage in Family Life Cycle (B^2=.032)			
Young, single	51	10	-119
Young, married, no children	54	223	284
Young, married, youngest child under 6	267	170	106
Young, married, youngest child 6 or older	110	274	125
Older, married, no children at home	110	-311	-211
Older, single	76	-426	-135
Any age, single, with children	72	-148	-127
Older, married, children at home	134	-81	-8
Major Change in Life Cycle (B^2=.015)			
Became single	46	9	114
Got married	45	284	339
Last child left home	31	105	110
No children to having children	32	148	-239
More than one change in marital status	13	-7	-53
No major change	707	-30	-22

NOTE: Mean outstanding installment debt = $764 (constant term); the R^2 for the regression was .210. There were 874 families in the regression analysis.

Appendix Table 7-3 (con't)

FAMILIES WITH AVERAGE ANNUAL INCOMES OF $10,000 OR MORE

Predictors	Number of Families	Unadjusted Deviations	Adjusted Deviations
Average Annual Income (B^2=.003)			
$10,000-12,499	253	47	30
$12,500-14,999	133	65	50
$15,000-19,999	86	-45	-26
$20,000 or more	63	-265	-192
Debt Attitude Index (B^2=.039)			
Very unfavorable attitudes	25	-630	-584
(Score of 2)	47	-583	-553
(Score of 3)	92	-39	-93
(Score of 4)	132	51	47
(Score of 5)	115	136	114
(Score of 6)	89	142	172
Very favorable attitudes	35	338	416
Change in Debt Attitude Index (B^2=.010)			
Less favorably inclined	79	-10	-166
Somewhat favorably inclined	107	-113	-170
No change	141	172	131
Somewhat more favorably inclined	119	66	97
More favorably inclined	89	-216	15
Stage in Family Life Cycle (B^2=.013)			
Young, single	12	-293	-437
Young, married, no children	31	209	153
Young, married, youngest child under 6	142	117	120
Young, married, youngest child 6 or older	97	31	128
Older, married, children at home	133	37	31
Older, married, no children at home	100	-246	-194
Older, single	8	-713	-543
Any age, single, with children	12	233	156
Major Change in Life Cycle (B^2=.006)			
Got married	9	182	343
Became single	11	-660	-489
Last child left home	39	100	51
No children to having children	12	438	266
More than one change in marital status	8	130	240
No major change	456	-10	-11

NOTE: Mean outstanding installment debt = $1182 (constant term); the R^2 for the regression was .025. There were 535 families in the regression analysis.

Chapter 8

CONCLUSIONS

In this volume we have focused on a number of variables which are known to be—or which economists have felt *should* be—important in determining how much individual households spend on consumer durables and the extent to which households use installment credit. Far from being exhaustive, the study provides but a brief introduction to the topics considered. In reexamining established relationships and considering some which are less well establihsed, what have we learned that is new? What implications do our findings have for the continued expansion of household capital formation and trends in consumer installment credit? What directions are suggested for new research?

The Demand for Consumer Durables

Chapter 2 considered the relation of expenditures on automobiles and major household durables to income. In contrast to cross-section analyses carried out earlier, Chapter 2 relates annual expenditures averaged over four consecutive years to the four-year, unweighted average of family income (after estimated federal income taxes). Relating average major expenditures to average income over an accounting period of several years provides an estimate of the cross-section relation that is relatively free of the biases which arise when shorter accounting periods are used. Short-run fluctuations in family income are averaged over a longer period of time, and as shown in Chapter 3, over several years the limited nature of the major expenditures variable tends to disappear. In addition, any individual year effects which might distort the shape of the static relation would tend to be averaged out.

The data in Chapter 2 show that expenditures on major durables equal the same proportion of income over much of the income distribution. However, even when averages over four years are used, expenditures as a proportion of income begin to decline at high income levels. The decline was very modest for families with average 1966-1969 incomes of between $10,000 and $15,000 a year. However, families with an average income over the four years of more than $15,000 spent from 1 to 3 percent less of their income on consumer durables than did middle income families—families with average 1966-1969 incomes between $5,000 and $10,000. While expenditures decline as a proportion of income at the upper end of the income distribution, the opposite is true for families at the bottom of the distribution. Although the panel is probably not a very good representation of the families at the low end of the distribution of income, the data in Chapter 2 do suggest that the proportion of income invested in major consumer durables rises a.; income increases, up to an income in 1966-1969 dollars of about $5,000.

The nonlinear relation of expenditures to income from the panel, and from other cross-section data as well, stands in marked contrast to the relation implied by the time series data shown in Chapter 1. Except for cyclical variations, expenditures on consumer durables have kept pace almost exactly with the growth in income over the postwar period, thus implying a linear proportionate relation between investments in major durables and income over that period. While there are a number of reasons why the simple cross-section and simple time series relations might legitimately appear inconsistent, the discrepancy does raise several issues regarding the process of generalizing from estimates derived from a cross-section at a point in time to changes over time.

In the past a major criticism of cross-section estimates has been that they are biased by errors in the measurement of independent variables. This criticism is particularly important for income where, for families with relatively high or relatively low observed incomes, the observed income may not reflect the family's normal income level, while the observed level of expenditures may. With several years of data, a number of alternative solutions to this problem are possible. The four-year unweighted average of income is the one used here.

A second problem encountered in assessing the validity of the cross-section relation is multicolinearity. This is a general problem encountered in estimating relations regardless of the type of data used. However, in the case of estimating the relation of expenditures to income there is reason to believe that correlates of income, rather than income itself, might lead to lower rates of expenditure on major durables at high and at low incomes. Thus, in assessing past trends and projecting future ones we would like to know if we can assert with some assurance that the factors leading to a decline in expenditures on major durables in a cross-section of families are factors that operate over time, or if the decline observed in the cross-section data is merely an illusion reflecting the particular characteristics of the families that at a given point in time are in the upper part of the income distribution.

In Chapter 4 we explored the differences in the demographic composition of families at different income levels. Families at different income levels are likely also to be in different stages of their earnings and family life cycle. Moreover, past analysis has shown that expenditures on major durables are related to family life cycle. However, to assess the possible impact of family life cycle on the distribution of expenditures within income categories, it is necessary to consider the joint distribution of family life cycle, income, and expenditures. An examination of the mean proportion of income spent on durables, distributed jointly within income and family life cycle groups, did not seem to indicate that family life cycle greatly distorted the effect of income on expenditures on major durables.

In addition, we recomputed the expenditure-income function for consumer durables, using dummy variable regression techniques for holding differences in family life cycle constant. For families with an average income below $5,000, the regression analysis did make some difference. For example, families with an income below $3,000 spent about 3 percent less of their incomes, after estimated federal income taxes, on major durables than did all panel families combined, before accounting for differences in family life cycle. They spent only about 2 percent less after taking account of family life cycle. For families with an average income in excess of $15,000, taking account of family life cycle made virtually no difference. These families spent between 1 and 2 percent less of their income on durables both before and after adjustment for other family characteristics. Thus, the general conclusion from this analysis was again that family life cycle and related family unit characteristics are insufficient to explain the major portion of the differences observed in the proportion of income that families at different income levels spend on automobiles and major household durables.

The analysis of Chapter 5 adds further credibility to the argument that, other things equal, as real income continues to rise we can expect families moving into new income classes to behave as those who currently occupy those classes. We feel that the measures of income trends over three years, developed for the analysis of Chapter 5, reflect permanent changes in income status fairly well. Although the analysis is subject to certain qualifications, there is no strong evidence that families who achieved new higher income status over the three years following the first panel interview, behaved differently from families having equivalent average incomes but whose income either did not change or fell somewhat over the period. Thus, families seem to adjust their expenditures on durables to new income levels quickly, and on average, adopt behavior similar to other families at that income level.

Overall, the evidence from the cross-section data indicates that the relation between expenditures on major consumer durables and income is not linear and that expenditure rates on major durables do fall at high levels of income. This assertion seems reasonable enough. Indeed, there seems to be no convincing reason to expect that families with greatly different incomes should spend the same proportion of these incomes on any particular commodity group. Yet the prediction that expenditure rates should eventually begin to decline as personal income rises has not been borne out over the postwar period. In the late 1960's and in the first two years of the 1970's, large numbers of families entered the income groups where our data suggest that a decline becomes marked in the proportion of income allocated to investments in consumer durables. But even during those years there is no evidence that the aggregate proportion of income allocated to consumer durables is falling. Why has the negative effect of large numbers of families entering the high income groups not been felt in the demand for durables? To what extent might it be felt in the near future?

On the basis of the data presented in this volume we cannot offer any solid answers to the above questions. The data do suggest, however, a number of factors that are likely to be important. We can see how these factors might best be incorporated into specific predictions. At least a part of the explanation for expenditures on major durables remaining roughly the same proportion of income, despite the rapid increase in the number of families in high income categories, probably lies in the cross-section relation itself. We note again that across the broad middle range of the income distribution, from $5,000 to almost $15,000, expenditures on durables are roughly the same proportion of income. Seventy-six percent of the families in the panel fell into this income range. Thus, at any given time the majority of families who experience changes in income may be expected to adjust their expenditures on durables by a fixed proportion of the change in income. Outside the broad middle range of the income distribution, however, the relation between expenditures and income is nonlinear at *both* ends of the distribution. Over the 1950's and 1960's the upward shift of income at all levels may have meant that the decline in expenditures as a proportion of income at high income levels was offset, all or in part, by the greater proportion of income spent on durables by families whose income rose from very low to not so low levels. In making future projections of the impact of income change on the rate of growth of expenditures on major durables, then, the decline in expenditures resulting from an increase in the proportion of families with an income of $15,000 or more (in constant 1966-1969 dollars) has to be balanced off against the increases in expenditures on durables by the movement of families with incomes below $5,000 into the middle income classes. Forecasters cannot just take changes in the average level of income, but should also examine concurrent changes in the total distribution of income.

While income is clearly the most important determinant of the demand for consumer durables, other things also matter. The cumulative impact of these other factors may more than offset any impact on investments in consumer durables, owing to changes in the level and distribution of income. As shown in Chapter 4, for example, while differences in the demographic composition of families at different income levels do not appear to distort dramatically the relation between expenditures on major durables and income, demographic characteristics do affect expenditure rates on durables. Of particular importance over the early postwar era may have been the rate of new household formation which increased during the 1950's and remained high throughout most of the 1960's. Of particular importance for the future may be the impact of recent trends in the proportion of single adult units and families with single female heads. Among the panel families it was found that single adult units spent on the average about 2 percent less of their income on major durables than did families with married heads. Families with single parents as their family head also spent 2 or more percent less of their income on durables. Any substantial increase in the proportion of family units with single heads—due to either later marriage or higher divorce rates—might tend to shift the expenditure-income function for major durables downward, reducing the proportion of income spent on durables at all income levels. Moreover, the lowered birth rates which currently prevail in the United States will lead to relatively smaller cohorts of young adults and young newly formed families in the future. This could eventually remove some of the cushion underlying new investments in consumer durables provided by the higher expenditure rates of young and recently formed families. In the panel, young married couples who had not yet had children spent between 1 and 2 percent more of their income on durables than did other married couples, and almost 4 percent more of their income on durables than families with single heads, regardless of their age.

Changes in the proportion of families at different stages in the family life cycle are likely to have some impact on household captial formation of all types. However, it is difficult to forecast the consequences of changes in the composition of the population on the demand for a specific group of commodities. Projecting movements in the life cycle distribution of the population is itself a difficult task which necessitates integrating a number of different demographic trends, including mortality, birth, marriage and divorce rates. Even were such projections readily available, we would be faced with the formidable task of integrating these projections with projections of the full distribution of income, which itself may be influenced by the distribution of families at different ages and in different marital states.[1]

---

[1] Guy Orcutt outlined a paradigm for studying the interaction and making projections of full distributions of variables. Orcutt's paradigm permits the types of nonlinearities observed in the relations which determine the demand for consumer durables. This paradigm is presented in "Microanalytic Models and Their Solution", an article in *Mathematical Model Building in Economics and Industry*, Charles Griffin and Company, Ltd., 1970. An early attempt to implement a simulation model of the type outlined by Orcutt is described in Guy H. Orcutt, et al., *Microanalysis of Socioeconomic Systems: A Simulation Study*, 1961.

Other factors also affect the level, though not necessarily the shape, of the expenditure-income function for consumer durables. Changes in the prices of consumer durables relative to other goods are almost impossible to study using cross-section data, or a cross-section time-series data base as short as four years. Changes here, however, will surely have some impact on the demand for durables, as will technological innovations and changes in the quality of durables. These factors may, of course, work in either direction, increasing or decreasing demand for consumer durables relative to other goods. Thus far, over the postwar period, durables have enjoyed a growing price advantage over many other goods. Prices of durables have risen less rapidly than other prices. The decline in the relative price of durables over the period may in part explain the lack of any noticeable decline in the proportion of aggregate personal income spent on major consumer durables. This decline has transpired despite the substantial growth in real income to current high levels. Such growth might be expected to place downward pressure on the proportion of income spent on durables. However, the relative advantage enjoyed by consumer durable goods producers may not continue. An example is the expected impact of new safety regulations on automobile prices.

Another factor which probably also helped maintain a high and growing level of demand for durables over the past 20 years is the steady growth in multiple car ownership. At all income levels multiple car ownership has risen. However, it may not be true that this impetus to growing demand will continue in the future. Suburbanization during the postwar period and a growing stock of relatively inexpensive used cars undoubtedly increased the demand for two or more cars per family. But increased urbanization and the development of alternative modes of transport may thwart any further tendency for more families to own two or more cars. There have been recent successes of a number of new communities which emphasize less reliance on the automobile as a mode of transport upon which all workers and housewives almost completely depend. This may signal a mood which de-emphasizes individually owned automobiles as the primary mode of transit used for all types of trips.

One other consideration seems worthy of careful study in assessing the longer-run growth of conventional consumer durables. Economists are inclined to ignore sociological considerations that might explain important differences between cross-section and time-series data and between short-run and longer-run movements in aggregates. There is by now ample evidence that values and differences in attitudes are often important factors underlying economic behavior. One such example is the discussion in Chapter 7 of attitudes toward installment credit and the use families make of such credit. Other examples are provided in recent research comparing the postwar experience of Germany, the United States, and Japan.[2]

If it is true that preference for different life styles accounts for substantial differences in the proportion of income spent on major durables by middle and upper income families, then, as the general level of income rises, the expected decline in the importance of consumer durables in the family budget will not occur without an accompanying change in values. Research now underway should increase our information about how values are associated with economic behavior. Such research should also increase our ability to make more appropriate links between values, economic behavior, and the movement of economic aggregates.[3] In addition, measuring attitudes toward different life styles may give helpful clues to changes in patterns of consumption. Such changes may influence either directly or indirectly the level and composition of the future demand for consumer durables regardless of the origins of such attitudes or the forces that cause them to change.

While Chapters 2 and 4 discussed the longer-run growth in the demand for automobiles and major household durables, the analysis of Chapters 5 and 6 was concerned primarily with temporary variations in the expenditure function over shorter periods of time. Two variables were examined in these chapters: trends in income and perceptions of past and expected changes in family financial well being.

There is no evidence that income trends, as measured in Chapter 5, led to accelerated rates of expenditure on major durables during 1966-69. Panel families with highly favorable trends spent no more on durables than families with unfavorable or no trends in income, once differences in the amount of income received by the family were taken into account. It is possible that in the very short run, changes in income do lead to accelerated rates of spending or to rapid cutbacks in spending at or near the turning points in business cycles. However, examination of the impact of trends in the income of individual families over three consecutive years (in which no major business cycle turning points occurred) discloses almost no evidence of an accelerator for expenditures on major durables even for families with very favorable income trends.

While calculated trends in income did not lead to major differences in expenditures from those expected on the basis of income alone, perceptions by families of changes in their personal financial situation did. Families with perceptions of favorable changes in their financial situation—feelings of being better off, and expectations of being still better off in the near future—

---

[2]See, for example, George Katona, Burkhard Strumpel, and Ernest Zahn, *Aspirations and Affluence: Comparative Studies in the United States and Western Europe,* 1971.

[3]A study underway at the Survey Research Center examines differences in values among socioeconomic groups. For preliminary findings, see Burkhard Strumpel, "Economic Life Styles, Values and Subjective Welfare—an Empirical Approach," a paper presented to 85th Annual Meeting of the American Economic Association, December, 1971.

spent proportionately more on major durables than did families who felt their situation was not getting better but staying pretty much the same. In turn, families who felt little change in their financial situation spent more on consumer durables, after taking account of income level, than families who thought their situation was clearly worsening or was going to worsen in the near future.

These findings indicate that attitudes are important in determining aggregate movements in consumer durable expenditures, as demonstrated by the correlation between the Survey Research Center's Index of Consumer Sentiment and short-run changes in expenditures on consumer durables. They also show that for individual families it is perception of financial progress rather than income change itself that is likely to be most important in influencing whether major discretionary expenditures, particularly on major consumer durables, occur at an accelerated rate.

The conclusion that subjective evaluation and expectations are more important than actual trends is strengthened by a set of preliminary experiments. These experiments—not reported in full detail in this volume—focused on the impact on expenditures for major durables of perceptions of financial progress in families with differing trends in income. The experiments showed that the amount by which the expenditures deviated from those expected, on the basis of perceptions of financial progress, was approximately the same regardless of whether the calculated trend in income was modest or quite large. Thus, having favorable attitudes and highly favorable actual income trends led to no greater spending than did having favorable attitudes and only moderately favorable trends in income. Although income trends and attitudes are correlated, the evidence here indicates that measuring income trends alone is not an adequate way to gauge consumer sentiment.[4]

Thus the findings of Chapters 5 and 6 of this volume add to the already

---

[4]The success of individual attitudes in predicting individual families' own levels of discretionary expenditures on durables in this study is interesting in light of the experience of past studies. Past studies which have related the attitudes of individual families to their own transaction levels have generally been inconclusive. We suggest that there are a number of reasons why our analysis appears more conclusive. First, with rare exceptions, past studies have had available only data on attitudes at a single point in time. Observations at a single point in time provide only a very limited amount of information regarding attitudes. The attitudes may have changed recently or they may have persisted for some time. They may or may not be firmly held. Having several observations, even when these observations are separated by fairly long intervals, such as one year, provides much more information concerning the attitudes themselves and their stability. Second, many things influence the major expenditures of a particular family in a given quarter or a single year. How long ago the family made its last car purchase, current installment debt obligations, and the overall liquidity position of the family are likely to be as important as recent changes in attitudes. Third, the limited nature of the major expenditures variable is likely to make it difficult to discriminate among important and less important predictors in an accounting period for major transactions as short as one year.

substantial evidence indicating that links between policy tools and behavior are not purely mechanical. The immediate impacts of changes in fiscal and monetary policy, and the time which it takes such impacts to be felt in the economy, do not depend solely upon that part of the economy, i.e., structure, which is currently captured in formal national income models. They also depend upon how such policy changes affect people's perceptions of their own personal situations and the situations of others around them. These chapters point out the obvious need to integrate more fully these attitudinal and financial data in making short-run forecasts.

The Growth of Consumer Installment Debt

The behavior of families with respect to the use of installment debt parallels in many ways the patterns observed in investments in consumer durables. As with expenditures on major durables, for example, installment debt balances decline as a proportion of income at high income levels. In other ways, the relationships are quite different. While the average number of dollars spent on durables continues to grow at even very high incomes, there is a sharp break in the relation of outstanding debt balances to income at an income level of about $10,000 a year. For families with an income less than $10,000, installment debt balances grow with income. Throughout this range installment debt is a constant proportion (about 12 percent) of income, except at the very bottom of the income distribution. At incomes above $10,000 but below $20,000 a year, outstanding installment debt is almost a constant amount, and hence declines rather rapidly as a proportion of income. At very high levels of income, $20,000 or more, installment debt balances begin to decline, not only relative to income but also in absolute amount.

The finding that families with moderately high incomes maintain lower installment debt balances relative to their incomes is not new, nor can it be shown that this cross-section observation is primarily the result of differences in characteristics other than income which are closely associated with income level. In Chapter 4, for example, it was shown that the use of installment debt is strongly influenced by family life cycle and its componenets. Moreover, it was shown that families in the panel with an average annual income of $10,000 or more were generally older and more established, with larger accumulations of financial assets which could be used to pay cash for even very large purchases. Despite the possible differences in ability to pay cash, and possible differences in time and liquidity preferences owing to differences in the life cycle composition of the various income groups, controlling for stage in the family life cycle and related family characteristics does little to change the basic relation of installment debt balances to income. Younger high income families use more debt than older high income families, but both use proportionately less installment debt than do middle income families. Thus, the cross-section data indicate that the growth in aggregate real income experienced over the postwar period should not have led to the unprecedented growth in installment debt which we witnessed. On the contrary, the steady growth of real income should have tended to discourage the rapid expansion of consumer installment credit.

Why has the downward pressure of income growth on installment debt expansion, expected on the basis of cross-section data, not materialized? To what extent might we expect income growth in the near future to thwart the further expansion of consumer credit?

In assessing the role of income in contributing to both the past and the expected future growth of investments in consumer durables, it seemed reasonable to assert that the cross-sectional relation between income and consumer durable investment expenditures has been nearly constant over the postwar period. Some cyclical variations have been seen and perhaps some upward drift due to favorable changes in the relative prices of durables and technological change in the durables sector. However, it is clear that the level of the relation between income and installment debt could not have been constant or even nearly so over the postwar period.

Using data from independently drawn cross-sections, the relation of mean outstanding installment debt to income was plotted in constant 1957-59 dollars for years between 1955 and 1969 (Chapter 2). Installment debt use among all but the lowest income groups increased markedly between 1955 and 1969. Moreover, a comparison of the relation of mean installment debt balances in 1965 and 1969 for families with similar incomes in constant dollars showed that the relation between installment debt use and income was still shifting upward and seemed to be doing so at about the same rate as in the latter half of the 1950's.[5]

The continued rapid upward shift of the income-installment-debt function over the latter half of the 1960's is sufficient to warn against making projections of the rate of growth of installment debt based primarily upon anticipated future income trends or on the basis of time-series relationships between income and installment debt. A stable or only slightly shifting installment debt function would not, of course, explain why the curve was shifting during the 1950's and early 1960's or why it had suddenly stopped shifting in the late 1960's. It would, however, have been an indication that those forces

---

[5]In one sense, explaining the instability of the debt-income function over the postwar period is quite simple. Four-year income explained fully 30 percent of the variance in the expenditures of panel families on major durables, and is by far the most important determinant of the average level of expenditures on major durables in both cross-section and time-series data. For installment debt, on the other hand, income explained only 17 percent of the variance in outstanding balances among panel families with an average income of less than $10,000 a year, and none of the variance in the outstanding installment debt balances of families with income of more than $10,000. Thus, while income and installment debt use are correlated, income is but one of a number of important determinants of installment debt use for families with incomes below $10,000 (in 1966-1969 dollars) and of no importance for families with higher incomes.

which had been leading to the changing installment debt use patterns by families at given levels of income were no longer operative, and that the depressing effect of income on installment debt use might be expected to be a stronger force in the demand for installment debt in the near future.

In the absence of stability in the debt-income relation, it becomes even more important to seek a further understanding of the forces other than income which affect the demand for consumer installment credit. Most students of consumer credit markets have emphasized factors on the supply side of the market, especially the liberalization of standards of credit worthiness and the introduction of longer maturities, as the major forces underlying the rapid growth of credit during the 1920's and the post-World War II era. In this study we have emphasized factors on the demand side of the consumer credit market.

Of the factors in addition to income studied in this volume, attitudes toward borrowing are clearly the most important. As shown in Chapter 7, even after taking account of other things which are correlated with attitudes toward installment debt use, differences in attitudes lead to striking differences in the amount of outstanding installment debt maintained by families. It can also be seen that although attainment of a certain income level does not lead to higher installment debt balances, the impact of attitudes toward debt use persists, even among families with high incomes.

In addition to the strong cross-sectional relation, the argument for the historical importance of changes in attitudes toward debt use in contributing to the growth in the demand for consumer installment credit over the 1960's, is strengthened by data from the archives of the Survey Research Center. A comparison of attitudes between 1959 and 1967 (Chapter 7) showed that Americans clearly became more favorably disposed toward borrowing between the late 1950's and the late 1960's. Comparisons of individual items included in the debt attitude index, developed in Chapter 7, showed that 20 percent more family heads approved of borrowing in 1967 than had done so in 1959, for at least some of the reasons listed. The strength of the correlation between attitudes and the use of installment debt, coupled with (1) the marked change in attitudes toward installment borrowing between 1959 and 1967, and (2) the substantial rate of growth of outstanding consumer installment debt over that period, all seem to indicate that attitudes toward installment debt use should be given careful consideration in predicting future movements in the use of installment debt.

While the evidence for including changes in consumer attitudes in projections of the growth of installment debt is convincing, their inclusion in productions is difficult, lacking information on the factors underlying the formation and changes of attitudes. Indeed, it is not possible, on the basis of the work included in this volume, to predict the future course of attitudes toward the use of installment debt. Nor are the data from the Consumer Panel Study particularly well-suited to studying changes in attitudes (though they are better suited than are data from a single cross-section with no reinterviews). The data presented here do, however, permit us to make some observations which we feel are important in evaluating the possible future course of attitudes and their continuing impact on the rate of growth of consumer installment credit. First, while many Americans now hold favorable attitudes, there is still much room for change in the direction of greater receptivity to borrowing. In 1967 only one-half of the heads of American families felt it was appropriate to borrow to finance the purchase of furniture; less than 10 percent felt it was appropriate to borrow to cover vacation expenses.

Second, a number of factors suggest that favorable changes in attitudes will continue to lead to increases in the use of installment debt. Americans are not now overcommitted in their installment debt obligations. Among panel families, for example, installment debt balances represented, on average, barely more than one month's income; only 11 percent of the families maintained average balances that equalled or exceeded four months of income; and few had trouble meeting their installment debt commitments. Indeed, even among those panel families who were most favorably disposed toward borrowing, mean average outstanding installment debt was less than 20 percent of average annual income.

On the asset side of the household balance sheet many American families are also in favorable positions. Many middle and upper-middle income families currently hold large amounts of equity in owner-occupied housing. While traditionally such equity has not been extensively used to finance major purchases, recent trends in the mortgage market seem to indicate an increasing willingness of families to use mortgage debt to finance non-housing expenditures. In addition, survey data show that even among families with installment debt, substantial liquid asset balances are not uncommon and often are in excess of the amount of the installment debt a family has outstanding.

A final factor that is likely to be highly compatible with translating changes in attitudes into actual increases in installment debt balances, is the current trend on the part of lending institutions, especially credit card agencies, to grant credit that is not associated with the acquisition of a specific asset. Any coupling of this trend with longer maturities on such debt might especially encourage the greater use of credit by families who have recently received or expect to receive substantial increases in income.

In short, there are several factors favorable to making attitudes a continuing important force underlying the rate of growth of consumer credit during the 1970's. There is considerable room for change in the direction of more favorable attitudes toward borrowing as a primary means of financing large outlays. A favorable balance sheet position is currently enjoyed by a majority of American families. There is a willingness of lending institutions to accomodate any increase in the demand for consumer installment credit.

While changes in attitudes toward borrowing are likely to remain one of the most important and most dynamic forces in the consumer credit market, they are by no means the only force. In Chapter 4 large differences in average outstanding installment debt balances were observed between families at different stages in the family life cycle. Young married couples who had not yet had a child maintained debt-to-income ratios about 5 percentage points higher than those maintained by young single people. In contrast, older married couples with no children under age 18 in the home maintained average debt-to-income ratios 5 percentage points lower than young married couples with no children.

We do not expect that demographic trends will lead to either rapid or substantial changes in expenditures on major durables in the near future, but rather that such changes would occur gradually over a long period of time. The differences in debt use among families at different stages in the life cycle are great enough, however, that even rather modest shifts in the demographic composition of families could conceivably exert considerable upward or downward pressure on the demand for consumer installment credit. Recent trends in the divorce rate, and the growth in the percentage of female headed households, plus any trend toward marrying later or not marrying at all, could exert downward pressure on the rate of growth of installment debt.[6]

While Chapters 2, 4, and 7 dealt with variables which are expected to dominate the longer-run trend in the demand for consumer installment debt, Chapters 5 and 6 considered the impact of two variables—income trends and perceptions and expectation of changes in financial well-offness—which are likely to influence short-run variations in the use of installment debt. Both calculated trends in income and respondents' evaluations of past and expected changes in their families' financial situations had some impact on the average installment debt balances maintained by families in the consumer panel. Favorable income trends and generally confident attitudes regarding personal financial progress led to more extensive use of installment debt. On the other hand, unfavorable income trends and general lack of confidence in financial progress were generally associated with less extensive installment debt use. However, while the impact of income trends *per se* was relatively weak, that of perceptions and expectations was very strong. In the final analysis, the families in the panel who were most pessimistic about personal financial progress in the

---

[6]As with expenditures on major durables, it is difficult to predict the net impact of changes in demographic distribution of the population on the rate of growth of installment debt in the near future. This is true if for no other reason than that our ability to predict trends in such demographic variables as family life cycle is still quite limited. As a part of a larger effort to study the impact of government policy, and changes therein, on the distribution of income, a population model is being developed at the Urban Institute which predicts not only the size of the population but also its demographic composition. For a brief description of the Urban Institute Model see Guy Orcutt, et al., *Microanalytic Simulation of Household Behavior,* Working Paper 504-5, The Urban Institute, Washington, D.C., September, 1971.

recent past and who generally lacked confidence about such developments in the near future, maintained installment debt balances that were on average $300 or more below the average balance of $923 for all families. Similarly, families who felt things were going well and who were confident that they would continue to go well, maintained average installment debt balances in excess of $300 above the average for all panel families. Especially noteworthy in the analysis is the strong impact on the use of installment debt of attitudes toward financial progress among families with an average income of $10,000 or more, families who were in the top 40 percent of the income distribution of the panel. Among this group of families, those who were highly confident and those who were generally pessimistic maintained average outstanding installment debt balances that differed by 20 percent or more from the average amount of debt held by all upper-middle income families.

The strength of the impact of perceived and expected financial progress is not surprising. Installment debt is, after all, a commitment made in the present on a stream of income to be accrued in the future. Confidence that the family is not likely to experience any financial setbacks in the near future is no doubt an essential element in the decision to borrow. Similarly, it is not surprising that the impact of income trends on installment debt balances is rather weak. Favorable past changes in income do not of necessity lead to confidence in the future, nor does the lack of highly favorable income trends necessarily mean that such changes cannot be expected soon. Indeed, since income trends (as defined in Chapter 5), and the index of financial progress (developed in Chapter 6), are positively correlated, the impact of income trends may largely reflect the strength of attitudes.

While the finding that use of installment debt by individual households is responsive to confidence in personal financial progress is neither surprising nor revolutionary, the finding has a number of implications for short-run economic stability which are worth exploring. The widespread use of installment credit by American families has stimulated speculation about whether this means of financing major transactions leads to excessive vulnerability of the household sector to business cycle changes. Another question is whether it fosters larger fluctuations in the economy that might otherwise be expected.

As stated earlier, at current levels of installment debt use most American families are in a position favorable not only to maintain current levels of debt but to sustain even higher levels of installment debt.[7] Thus, for downturns of

---

[7]The growth in bankruptcies has been viewed with alarm by many analysts. However, it is important to note that filing for bankruptcy is still a relatively rare phenomenon and that only small numbers of increases in absolute levels of bankruptcy cases lead to very large percentage changes in total bankruptcies filed. Moreover, the increase in bankruptcies is not necessarily a sign of excessive and immoderate use of installment debt or even of a growth in the proportion of families who badly manage their finances. Rather, increases in bankruptcy suits may reflect a more widespread knowledge of the possibility of filing for bankruptcy and the probable gains of doing so. Also, the growth of bankruptcies may be an indication of the increased availability and more extensive use of legal counsel by all socio-economic groups.

the magnitude experienced during the latter half of the postwar period, there would seem to be no immediate danger that a major portion of the families in the country would find themselves in serious financial jeopardy. Inevitably, some families will find themselves unexpectedly in unfortunate circumstances whenever the rate of unemployment rises, and families who have debt may be temporarily worse off than those with no debt. The fact remains, however, that the household sector seems in no imminent danger of total collapse, even were a rather severe recession to occur.

Furthermore, the fact that many American families maintain outstanding installment debt balances equal to two or more months of income, probably does little to exacerbate a downturn, once started. A lack of confidence will lead to a decline in the rate of growth of new credit extensions, which might not occur if installment debt were not so widely used. However, a general decline in confidence would lead to the postponement of major purchases, regardless of how these purchases were financed.

The widespread use of installment debt, its expected even wider use in the future, and the responsiveness of installment debt balances to changes in consumer confidence, are potentially more destabilizing on an upswing than at a downturn. With the widespread acceptance and use of installment debt, a given liquid asset base can support an expansion of purchases several times larger than the asset base itself. Thus, favorable changes in consumer confidence can quickly make themselves felt in the market place and, potentially at least, can be highly inflationary.

While the data presented here strongly suggest that sharp changes in attitudes toward financial progress could lead to rapid expansions of installment debt and to purchases related to this expansion, there are also indications that any such expansion would tend to be self-regulating. Even families who were very optimistic, and whose optimism persisted without interruption for the several years of the panel, were not likely to maintain excessively high installment debt balances relative to income. When asked whether they could easily carry more debt than they now have, families in the panel, like families interviewed previously in the Survey of Consumer Finances, were able to respond to the question easily and readily, indicating that they have fairly clear-cut notions about how much installment debt they can comfortably carry. Moreover, responses to quesions about whether they could easily carry more debt were closely associated with the amount of debt they currently held, those holding large amounts of debt being more likely to respond that they could not easily incur new debt without first reducing the amount they currently had.

Other data collected by the Survey Research Center also suggest that any increase in the rate of inflation due to a rapid expansion of purchases on credit would tend to reduce further expansion in the household sector. Americans, who expect continued inflation at a low rate, view increases in the rate of inflation very pessimistically and, apparently believing that the only way to beat inflation is not to spend, respond by checking major expenditures rather than purchasing in anticipation of further rapid inflation.

It cannot be denied that the widespread use of installment debt and the responsiveness of installment debt use to changes in consumer confidence could lead to more fluctuations in consumer spending than would be the case if major transactions were financed largely from accumulated liquid assets. Yet, our current knowledge of consumer behavior indicates that such destabilizing effects are largely self-regulating and non-accelerating.

Further Research

The analysis of this volume could be extended in several directions using the data from the four-year consumer panel study. In this volume we have considered separately expenditures on major consumer durables and outstanding installment debt. These two variables could easily be incorporated into a broader analysis. Several analysts have argued that much of the capital expansion in the consumer investment goods sector since the early 1920's is due to the liberalization and growth of consumer installment credit. It is difficult to prove or disprove this assertion, but it may shed some light to consider jointly the investment and installment debt decision for individual families.

Is it true, for example, that people with more favorable attitudes toward installment debt not only use more installment debt, but also spend more on automobiles and other major durables? Or do more favorable attitudes toward installment debt merely lead to financing an increased proportion of a predetermined amount of expenditures with installment debt rather than with liquid assets? In carrying out such experiments it would, of course, be necessary to take carefully into account factors that would be associated with both higher installment debt and higher rates of expenditure on major durables.

We have also restricted the analysis of this volume to longer-run, static relations and, in general, to the factors which might cause these relations to change over time. Only passing attention has been given to shorter-run variations in the relations considered, to the process by which families adjust their stocks of installment debt and consumer durables, and to the factors which influenced the timing of the total purchases of each family observed over the four years. Yet, the panel data are well-suited to studying short-run changes and the impact of past decisions on subsequent behavior. With two years of data on the same families, a decision can be related not only to the current status of the household, but also to the position of the household at the beginning of the period. With four years of data, lagged values and changes over two previous periods can be related to behavior in the current period.

There is a rather natural framework for the various components of the expenditures and installment debt decisions, and the shorter- and longer-run implications of these decisions. This framework is the stock adjustment type model used by Chou in studying the demand for automobiles using aggregated time-series data and later by Watts and Tobin using household data. A generalized stock adjustment framework for analyzing household behavior was outlined by Zellner in 1960 at the Conference on Consumption and Saving.

The Consumer Panel Study data are well-suited for analysis within the stock adjustment framework. Measures of most important stocks in the family portfolio are either available directly from the basic coded data or can be derived from them. A recent article by Dunkelberg and Stafford used the data from the first two years of the panel to fit a stock adjustment model of changes in outstanding installment debt over one year. The analysis of this volume suggests that the analysis of Dunkelberg and Stafford could be expanded to include other factors. Debt attitudes could be introduced either singly or in combination with other variables to add liquidity preferences as a variable in determining equilibrium stock values for individual households. Debt attitudes would then become important in determining desired stocks of installment debt and also desired levels of liquid and other types of assets. The analyses of Chapters 5 and 6 also suggest that attitudes, such as the variance in the attitudes of individual families around their own average, for example, could be introduced. Also, the average change in attitudes across all families might also be expected to affect the adjustment coefficients for a particular year.

A third extension of the analysis present in this volume would be to disaggregate the major dependent variables and analyze their components. While it is total spending on major discretionary items which is most important in determining short-run movements in consumer demand, changes in the demand for each individual component will be important in determining the general trend in aggregate expenditures on conventional consumer durables. Of particular importance are investments in and the consumption of automobiles. The panel includes extensive data on the ownership of cars, purchases of cars on a calendar year basis, and the total value of cars owned at each time the family unit was interviewed. Also, some measures of urbanization are available in addition to the extensive data on other demographic and family characteristics. These data would permit studies of the demand for automobiles, the timing of purchases, and change and trends in either the number of cars owned or the value of the total car stock.

Average outstanding installment debt balances are jointly determined by the amount borrowed and the length of time over which the loan is to be repaid. As shown in Chapter 2, the ratio of monthly payments to outstanding installment debt balances is fairly similar across all income groups, indicating about the same average maturity. However, between families maturities vary considerably. A separate study of the monthly payments constraint and of preferences for different maturities would further increase our knowledge of how families are likely to respond to changes on the supply side of the credit market and of what types of change would illicit the greatest response.

Appendix A

INTERCORRELATION OF MAJOR VARIABLES

Appendix Table A-1 (Sheet 1 of 3)

INTERCORRELATION OF MAJOR VARIABLES

All Panel Families

	$\bar{E}$	E/Y	$\bar{D}$	D/Y	$\bar{Y}$	dY/dt($)	dY/dt(%)	IFP	IDA	AGE	A&R	A&R/Y
$\bar{E}$	1.0											
E/Y	.73	1.0										
$\bar{D}$	.38	.30	1.0									
D/Y	.22	.37	.86	1.0								
$\bar{Y}$	.51	-.04	.21	-.09	1.0							
dY/dt($)	.14	.05	.11	.06	.14	1.0						
dY/dt(%)	.06	.06	.07	.08	-.01	.81	1.0					
IFP	.22	.12	.22	.17	.20	.19	.17	1.0				
IDA	.10	.11	.18	.17	.05	-.01	-.02	.10	1.0			
AGE	-.02	-.11	-.17	-.22	.08	-.15	-.23	-.31	-.12	1.0		
A&R	.25	.04	.20	.07	.35	.09	.03	.06	.01	.03	1.0	
A&R/Y	.09	.07	.13	.10	.05	.03	.01	-.04	-.02	.04	.85	1.0

DEFINITIONS: $\bar{E}$ is four-year average annual expenditures on major durables. E/Y is proportion of four-year income after taxes spent on major durables. $\bar{D}$ is average beginning of year installment debt balances. D/Y is ratio of average outstanding installment debt to four-year average annual income. DY/dt($) is income trend in dollars per year. DY/dt(%) is income trend in percent per year. IFP is index of past and expected financial progress. IDA is index of debt attitudes. AGE is age of the family head at the time of the initial interview. A&R is average annual expenditures on additions and repairs to the home. A&R/Y is ratio of average expenditures on additions and repairs to average annual income. For additional explanations of the definitions and derivations of the variables see the chapter in which each is discussed.

Appendix Table A-1 (Sheet 2 of 3)

INTERCORRELATION OF MAJOR VARIABLES

Average Annual Income Less than $10,000

	$\bar{E}$	E/Y	$\bar{D}$	D/Y	$\bar{Y}$	dY/dt($)	dY/dt(%)	IFP	IDA	AGE	A&R	A&R/Y
$\bar{E}$	1.0											
E/Y	.89	1.0										
$\bar{D}$	.48	.36	1.0									
D/Y	.40	.39	.94	1.0								
$\bar{Y}$	.50	.18	.42	.22	1.0							
dY/dt($)	.16	.10	.22	.18	.20	1.0						
dY/dt(%)	.07	.06	.12	.12	.03	.88	1.0					
IFP	.21	.16	.27	.24	.25	.22	.17	1.0				
IDA	.14	.12	.19	.17	.15	.02	-.01	.14	1.0			
AGE	-.18	-.14	-.24	-.23	-.18	-.25	-.24	-.38	-.14	1.0		
A&R	.18	.09	.15	.10	.24	-.01	-.05	-.01	-.03	.04	1.0	
A&R/Y	.09	.08	.08	.07	.08	-.03	-.04	-.08	-.05	.10	.92	1.0

DEFINITIONS:　see Sheet 1 of Table A-1

Appendix Table A-1 (Sheet 3 of 3)

INTERCORRELATION OF MAJOR VARIABLES

Average Annual Income $10,000 or More

	E	E/Y	D̄	D/Y	Ȳ	dY/dt($)	dY/dt(%)	IFP	IDA	AGE	A&R	A&R/Y
E	1.0											
E/Y	.83	1.0										
D̄	.23	.28	1.0									
D/Y	.17	.34	.93	1.0								
Ȳ	.28	-.20	.00	-.21	1.0							
dY/dt($)	.02	.03	.02	.01	.00	1.0						
dY/dt(%)	.04	.07	.02	.03	-.07	.89	1.0					
IFP	.11	.07	.13	.10	.07	.15	.17	1.0				
IDA	.02	.09	.17	.18	-.08	-.06	-.04	.02	1.0			
AGE	.04	-.03	-.16	-.19	.12	-.16	-.21	-.26	-.10	1.0		
A&R	.13	-.01	.16	.10	.23	.06	.11	.04	.01	-.06	1.0	
A&R/Y	.06	.04	.19	.19	-.01	.07	.11	.02	.04	-.10	.93	1.0

DEFINITIONS: see Sheet 1 of Table A-1

Appendix B

NON-INSTALLMENT DEBT USERS

Many American families cannot make major expenditures on household durables without making some adjustment in their economic behavior. One such adjustment is taking a second job or having a secondary earner enter the labor force. Another alternative is re-evaluation of asset balances and saving rates; by saving less or by reducing liquid asset balances households can free funds. A third alternative—the one most prevalent among households in America—is to expand current income through the use of installment credit. This appendix contrasts the subgroup of families in the 1967-1970 Consumer Panel who were debt-free throughout the entire four years of the study with those who were not.[1]

As shown in the tabulation below, 19 percent or approximately one out of every five panel families did not use installment debt over four consecutive years.

Ratio of Outstanding Installment Debt to Income (in percent)	Proportion of Families
No debt	19
0.1-4.9	21
5.0-9.9	18
10.0-14.9	15
15.0-24.9	16
25.0 or more	11
Total	100

[1]Families who had no outstanding installment debt at the time of any of the four interviews are classified as non-installment debt users here. It is possible that some small percentage of these families may have incurred and retired debt between interviews.

The other 81 percent of the families who did maintain non-zero outstanding installment debt balances, of course, varied widely in amount of debt held relative to income. While 21 percent of the families maintained balances that did not exceed 5 percent of their average annual income, 27 percent maintained outstanding balances equal to 15 percent or more of their income. What factors explain why some families used installment debt not at all, while other families used some installment debt, and still others used installment debt extensively?

The tabulation below shows the relative importance of various family characteristics in predicting whether the family would use some installment debt or none at all.

In a multivariate analysis of debt and non-debt use, the most powerful predictor of whether a family would use installment debt was the proportion of income allocated to purchases of cars and major household durables over the 4 years. While it was found that non-debt users were certainly not non-spenders, almost half again as many debtors had relatively high expenditure to income ratio (10 percent or more) as did non-debtors. The proportions were 41 percent and 28 percent, respectively.

The relative importance of all of the predictors included in the multivariate analysis is shown below:

Family Characteristic	Relative Importance (Beta Coefficients)
Proportion of four-year income spent on major durables	.154
Average annual income	.137
Age of head	.132
Index of debt attitudes	.098
Index of financial progress	.087
Marital status	.065
Housing status	.057

The predictors are ranked according to the beta coefficients ("partial R^2s") obtained from a dummy variable regression of the type used elsewhere in this volume (see Chapter 4 for a brief description of the program).

Average annual income was the second most important factor distinguishing non-users from installment debt users. As shown in Appendix Table B-1, non-installment debt users are more frequent at the extremes of the income distribution. The income distribution of non-debtors shows that these households consist both of families for whom credit is not available or available only at a high cost, and families for whom debt financing is neither necessary nor a particularly attractive means of financing major purchases.

Age as a predictor of debtor status had about the same relative importance as did average annual income. The age distribution of debtors and non-debtors is also shown in Appendix Table B-1. Young families whose heads are under 35 years old compose a much larger percentage of debtors than they do of non-debtors—37 percent and 17 percent, respectively. In contrast, almost 50 percent of all non-debtors are 50 years old or older, while only 20 percent of families who had some outstanding installment debt balances were headed by persons 50 years old or older.[2]

Although not as important as age and income, the two major attitudinal variables included in the analysis of this volume ranked high as predictors of whether a family made use of installment credit. Among those families who had no outstanding installment debt at the time of any of the four panel interviews, 26 percent had clearly unfavorable attitudes toward borrowing as a method of financing unusual expenditures. Only half as large a proportion of installment debt users had such unfavorable attitudes. Judging from the analysis of Chapter 7, the impact of these attitudes would undoubtedly have been strengthened had changes in attitudes toward the use of installment credit been included as well. As with families who viewed borrowing negatively, families who were pessimistic about their financial progress over the course of the four years in which the panel interviews were taken were less likely to be users of installment debt than were families who were optimistic. While 40 percent of non-debtors had zero or negative scores on the index of financial progress, as shown in Appendix Table B-1, only 24 percent of debt users were so pessimistic about recent and expected changes in their financial situation.

Appendix Table B-2 presents the results of an analysis of installment debt use using a multivariate search technique. Beginning with all families, the program searches for the best bivariate division of the sample on each of a set of prespecified categorical predictors. Each of the predictors may have up to 10 categories. When the best single split—defined in terms of the variance explained—is found, each of the subgroups is re-examined individually and independently to find the best bivariate division for the subgroup—where the best split is again defined as the one which explains the most variance in the dependent variable, in this case whether the family used installment debt.[3]

---

[2]Families with heads aged 60 or older were excluded from the panel in the initial interview. Thus the "50 or over" age category is composed almost entirely of families whose head is in the labor force.

[3]For a detailed description of the procedure and program used to produce Appendix Table B-2 see John Sonquist and James Morgan, *The Detection of Interaction Effects,* the Institute for Social Research, Ann Arbor, Michigan, 1964. A more recent and more flexible version of this same basic technique is described in Sonquist, et al., *Searching for Structure (Alias-AID-III),* the Institute for Social Research, 1971.

The percentages appearing in each of the boxes in Appendix Table B-2 relate the number of families not using installment debt to the total number of families in the subgroup defined by the box. All of the predictors included in the earlier multivariate analysis were included in the analysis presented in Appendix Table B-2.

While expenditure rates on major durables and income were the most important predictors of whether a family had outstanding installment debt balances in a dummy variable regression, the multivariate search program showed that whether the family head was under or over 50 years old was the most important distinction between installment debt users and non-users. One-third of the families with heads aged 50 or older had no outstanding installment debt at the time of any of the four panel interviews, while only 13 percent of the families with younger heads had no outstanding installment debt at the time of the first interview and incurred no installment debt over the course of the next three years.

Among households with heads over 50 years of age, the majority of those with an average annual income of less than $3,000, or of $15,000 or more, did not have or incur installment debt over four consecutive years. On the other hand, middle income older families were as likely to use installment debt as families with heads under 50 years old, provided they were highly optimistic about their personal financial progress. Middle income older families who were not highly optimistic about changes in their personal financial situation, however, were much less inclined to take on installment debt and were especially unlikely to do so if they had unfavorable attitudes toward borrowing.

Among families with heads under age 50 at the time of the first interview, there was a small group of 18 families who made no major purchases of cars or household durables over four years. Most of these families also did not have any outstanding installment debt over that period. For families who made at least one major purchase, whether the family head was over or under age 40 was important in determining whether the family bought on credit. Those whose heads were between ages 40 and 50 used credit less frequently. Although there were a substantial number of families with heads under age 40 in the panel, installment debt is so widespread among these families that no single bivariate division of the sample on any of the predictors included in the analysis could meaningfully distinguish any subgroup here as being substantially more or less likely to be non-installment debt users.

As in the case of middle income families with heads over age 50, the single most important deterrent of installment debt use among families with heads between the ages of 40 and 49 was perceptions and expectations regarding personal financial progress. Highly pessimistic families were twice as likely not to use installment debt as moderately optimistic or highly optimistic families.

In general the analysis presented in Appendix Table B-2 suggests that for older families income is a more important determinant of whether a family uses installment debt, than it is for younger families. Particularly for families with middle and late-middle aged heads, feelings about past and probable future changes in personal financial situation are important considerations in whether the family takes on installment debt obligations. In addition it appears that, while rates of expenditure on major durables are the most important determinant of installment debt use in a dummy variable regression analysis, expenditure rates are less important than other things after the sample is divided into age groups.

Appendix Table B-1

CHARACTERISTICS OF FAMILIES WHO DID NOT USE INSTALLMENT CREDIT
OVER FOUR CONSECUTIVE YEARS

(Percentage Distribution)

Characteristic	All Families	Non-Installment Debt Users	Installment Debt Users
Average Annual Income			
Less than $3,000	6	12	4
$3,000-4,999	8	10	8
$5,000-7,499	22	17	23
$7,500-9,999	27	19	29
$10,000-14,999	27	25	27
$15,000 or more	10	17	9
Total	100	100	100
Age of Head[1]			
Under 30	20	12	22
30-39	26	12	29
40-49	27	29	27
50 or older	27	47	22
Total	100	100	100
Debt Attitude Index[1]			
Highly unfavorable attitudes			
(Score of 2)	6	11	5
(Score of 3)	9	15	8
(Score of 4)	16	18	16
(Score of 5)	26	23	26
(Score of 6)	17	12	18
Highly favorable attitudes	4	3	5
Total	100	100	100
Index of Financial Progress			
Highly pessimistic	4	7	4
(-1 and -2)	10	16	9
(0)	12	17	11
(1 - 3)	35	32	34
(4 and 5)	21	16	22
(6 and 7)	14	9	15
Highly optimistic	4	3	5
Total	100	100	100
Number of Families	1436	267	1169

[1]At the time of the first interview with the family unit in early 1967.

Table B-2

PROPORTION NOT USING INSTALLMENT DEBT

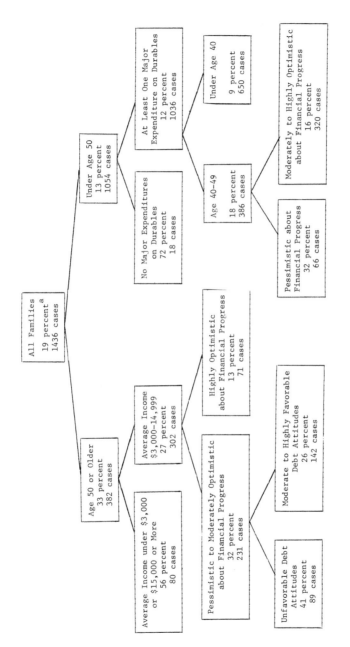

All Families
19 percent[a]
1436 cases

Age 50 or Older
33 percent
382 cases

Under Age 50
13 percent
1054 cases

Average Income under $3,000
or $15,000 or More
56 percent
80 cases

Average Income
$3,000-14,999
27 percent
302 cases

At Least One Major
Expenditure on Durables
12 percent
1036 cases

No Major Expenditures
on Durables
72 percent
18 cases

Pessimistic to Moderately Optimistic
about Financial Progress
32 percent
231 cases

Highly Optimistic
about Financial Progress
13 percent
71 cases

Under Age 40
9 percent
650 cases

Age 40-49
18 percent
386 cases

Unfavorable Debt
Attitudes
41 percent
89 cases

Moderate to Highly Favorable
Debt Attitudes
26 percent
142 cases

Moderately to Highly Optimistic
about Financial Progress
16 percent
320 cases

Pessimistic about
Financial Progress
32 percent
66 cases

[a]This percentage relates the number of families not using installment debt to the total number in the subgroup defined in the box.

Appendix C

EXTREME OBSERVATIONS

Included in the Consumer Panel are 30 families who reported spending more than 25 percent of their income on cars and major household durables, and 27 families who maintained outstanding installment debt balances equal to 50 percent or more of their average annual income. Although the behavior of these families is in many instances reasonable, they are excluded from much of the analysis of this volume. With a small sample of families, extreme observations tend to dominate the average of any subgroup into which they happen to fall. Least squares regressions are used frequently throughout the analysis to test the significance and magnitude of the impact of important variables upon expenditures for major durables and installment debt balances. Therefore, to include these few very different cases is to risk markedly distorting the regression estimates. By excluding these few families, however, we do not risk obscuring the pattern of economic behavior found among the majority of families.

Families who were judged to be either extreme spenders or to hold extremely large amounts of installment debt relative to their incomes, are compared to all panel families on a number of different characteristics in Appendix Table C-1.

Families with expenditure rates on major durables of 25 percent or more of their income differ from other panel families in two important respects: their age and their propensity to purchase automobiles. Families who over four years spent 25 percent or more of their income on major durables were, on average, about eight years younger than those families who spent less than 25 percent on these items. As shown in Appendix Table C-1, 16 (or 53 percent) of the 30 families who were extremely big spenders had heads under age 30 at the time of the first interview. In contrast, only 20 percent of all of the families in the panel had heads under age 30 at that time.

Of the 30 families classified as big spenders, 19 made three or more car purchases over the course of the four years of the panel, and this group of families were three times as likely to purchase three or more cars than were families in the panel who spent less than 25 percent of their income on major durables. Moreover, none of the families classified as extreme spenders on durables made no car purchase over the four years and only three families in this group purchased only one car.

Completing the profile of very big spenders, we find that these families were much more likely to be single or newly married than were other panel families. In addition these families were, on the one hand, more likely to have an average annual income of under $5,000, and, on the other, were more likely to have experienced trends in income over the four-year period of 15 percent or more per year. Indeed, 10 out of the 30 families had trends in income of 20 percent or more per year. Families with expenditures equal to or exceeding 25 percent of their income were neither overwhelmingly more nor overwhelmingly less optimistic about their financial progress than other panel families, nor were these families overwhelmingly enthusiastic about the use of installment debt.

Families who maintained very high installment debt balances relative to their incomes are as likely to have been classified "extreme" because of idiosyncrasies in the definition of installment debt as they are for having extraordinary amounts of installment debt. As in the annual Survey of Consumer Finances, debt incurred for the purchase of house trailers is not classified as mortgage debt, but rather as installment debt along with such debt as is incurred for the purchase of automobiles, washing machines, etc. An examination of the interviews of families with installment debt to income ratios of 50 percent or more revealed that approximately half of the 27 families with such high debt to income ratios had house trailer debt. If this debt had been classified as mortgage debt, or classified separately from debt incurred for nonhousing items, these families would have had debt to income ratios within the range considered acceptable to be included in the analyses of Chapters 2-7.

Of the remaining half of the families with extreme outstanding installment debt balances, two had very low incomes. One family, headed by a farmer, had an income ranging from $1,300 to $2,200 in each of the four years and the only installment debt held by this family was for a jeep. The other family, headed by a woman and including her child and several grandchildren, had an income per year ranging from $100 to $1100 and a large house repair loan. The 12 remaining families had moderate incomes and their installment debt loans were related to standard durable items, but simply were very large relative to those of the panel as a whole. These families did not seem to differ from other panel families in any notable respect, nor did they have in common any particular characteristic that might have explained why they maintained such high average outstanding installment debt balances relative to their incomes.

There is little overlap between families who had very high rates of expenditure on major durables and families with ratios of installment debt to income of 50 percent or more. Only four families fell in both the extreme expenditure and the extreme installment debt group.

Appendix Table C-1

CHARACTERISTICS OF FAMILIES WITH EXTREME EXPENDITURE RATES
AND UNUSUALLY HIGH INSTALLMENT DEBT TO INCOME RATIOS

(Percentage Distribution and Frequencies)

Demographic Characteristic	Proportion of All Panel Families	Expenditure to Income Ratio of 25 Percent or More		Debt to Income Ratio of 50 Percent or More	
		Proportion	Number of Families	Proportion	Number
Average Annual Income					
Under $5,000	14	40	12	22	6
$5,000-9,999	49	47	14	70	19
$10,000-14,999	27	13	4	4	1
$15,000 or more	10	–	0	4	1
Total	100	100	30	100	27
Age of Head					
Under 30	20	53	16	37	10
30-39	26	13	4	26	7
40-49	27	17	5	15	4
50-55	27	17	5	22	6
Total	100	100	30	100	27
Stage in Family Life Cycle					
Young, single	3	17	5	–	0
Young, married, no children	4	13	4	7	2
Young, married, youngest child under 6	22	33	10	34	9
Young, married, youngest child 6 or older	18	10	3	26	7
Older, married, children at home	20	10	3	7	2
Older, married, no children at home	19	7	2	15	4
Older, single	8	7	2	4	1
Any age, single with children	6	3	1	7	2
Total	100	100	30	100	27
Income Trend (percent per year)					
-5.0 percent or less	12	14	4	11	3
0.0 to -4.9	10	20	6	15	4
0.1 to 4.9	17	3	1	11	3
5.0 to 9.9	22	10	3	15	4
10.0 to 14.9	16	13	4	7	2
15.0 percent or more	23	40	12	41	11
Total	100	100	30	100	27

Appendix Table C-1 (con't)

Demographic Characteristic	Proportion of All Panel Families	Expenditure to Income Ratio of 25 Percent or More		Debt to Income Ratio of 50 Percent or More	
		Proportion	Number of families	Proportion	Number
Years Married					
2 or fewer	19	40	12	15	4
3-4	4	17	5	15	4
5-9	13	20	6	11	3
10-19	27	3	1	33	9
20 or more	37	20	6	26	7
Total	100	100	30	100	27
Index of Financial Progress					
Pessimistic	14	13	4	8	2
(0)	12	13	4	7	2
(1 to 3)	35	27	8	52	14
(4 and 5)	21	27	8	15	4
Optimistic	18	20	6	18	5
Total	100	100	30	100	27
Number of Cars Purchased in Calendar Years 1966-1969					
None	19	–	0	8	2
One	35	10	3	44	12
Two	25	27	8	22	6
Three	13	40	12	26	7
Four or more	8	23	7	–	0
Total	100	100	30	100	27
Debt Attitude Index					
Unfavorable	15	13	4	8	2
(Score of 3)	16	7	2	15	4
(Score of 4)	26	20	6	37	10
(Score of 5)	22	23	7	15	4
Favorable	21	37	11	25	7
Total	100	100	30	100	27
Number of Families	1436	30	30	27	27

NOTE: Stage in family life cycle and years married are at the time of the final interview in early 1970. Age of head and debt attitudes are at the time of the initial interview with the family in early 1967.

Appendix D

PANEL MORTALITY

All who venture to collect and analyze sample survey data confront the problem of nonresponse and the possible accompanying biases. The problem is particularly acute for panel studies where movers often cannot be located and families experiencing financial difficulties may be reluctant to grant reinterviews. The analysis in this volume is based largely upon the data obtained from a reinterview study conducted by the Survey Research Center. Under a grant from the Ford Foundation, four interviews were sought with the same families between early 1967 and early 1970 at intervals of approximately 12 months. The original sample consisted of a national cross-section, excluding Alaska and Hawaii, of heads of primary family units who were under age 60 at the time of the first interview in early 1967. Thus, families whose heads were 60 years old or older in early 1967 and secondary family units are excluded from the study.[1]

In early 1967, 2,604 families were interviewed who qualified to be reinterviewed for the subsequent waves of the panel study. When interviewing was completed in early 1968, only 1,921 families or 74 percent of the eligible families remained. Some families refused to be interviewed a second time, while some who moved could not be followed. A few families could not be found at home at any time during the interviewing period or could not be located for other reasons. After the third interviewing period, in early 1969, 1,569 families remained in the panel and of these 1,441 could be located and granted a

---

[1] A family unit is defined as all persons living in the same dwelling unit who are related to each other by blood, marriage or adoption. A single person who is unrelated to other occupants of a dwelling, or who lives alone, is a family unit by himself. When more than one family occupies a dwelling unit, the primary unit is the one who owns the dwelling or pays the rent. In the case of joint ownership or rent payment, the unit with the largest income or the oldest head is designated the primary unit.

fourth interview in early 1970. Thus, of the 2,604 families who qualified to be interviewed after the completion of the first wave of data collection, only 1,441 (55 percent) completed all four interviews.

This appendix compares the families who remained in the panel in early 1970 after the fourth interview with an independent cross-section of families interviewed during the first and second quarters of 1970 and with the 2,604 families interviewed in early 1967 who qualified to remain in the panel.

The Panel Compared to an Independent Cross-Section

In early 1970 a cross-section of newly drawn households was interviewed for the annual Survey of Consumer Finances. Excluding secondary families and families whose heads were over age 62, the newly drawn Survey of Consumer Finances sample may be used as a standard against which to measure the representatives of the subgroup of 55 percent of the original panel families, who completed all of the four interviews between early 1967 and early 1970.

As shown in Appendix Table D-1, the final panel remains remarkably representative on the basis of a large number of demographic and financial variables despite the overall response rate of only 55 percent. In fact, the differences observed between the distribution of panel members and the 1970 Survey of Consumer Finances cross-section are probably largely the result of the exclusion of split-offs from the panel rather than differential response rates among demographic subgroups.

No attempt was made in the panel to include members of households in the original sample who, during the course of the panel, left the nuclear family to establish family units of their own. Thus the under-representation of young families in the final panel. The decision not to follow split-offs from the original family unit, in turn, may explain in part the difference observed in the income distributions in Appendix Table D-1.

The difference between percentage of households headed by a male in the panel years versus that of the 1970 cross-section is the result of lower response rates among households headed by females.

In Appendix Table D-2 the joint distribution of age and education is compared for the panel and the 1970 Survey of Consumer Finances. Here again there is a remarkable similarity between the two distributions despite the large panel losses.

Response Rates by Demographic Characteristic

In Appendix Table D-3, distributions of families who completed the first in the series of four interviews are compared with those for families who completed all of the interviews. In addition, in the last column of the table response rates are computed for each of the subgroups shown.

Some of the largest differences in response rates are found among income groups. For families with an income of $15,000 or more in 1966 response rates are 20 percent higher than for families with an income of less than $5,000 in 1966. Hence, while nearly 82 percent of the final panel families earned $5,000 or more in 1966, 78 percent of the original sample of families who completed the first interview earned $5,000 or more in that year. The bias caused by the loss of relatively more low-income families, however, produced a difference in mean 1966 income between the two groups of families of only $613 ($9,816 vs. $9,203).

While there are fairly substantial differences in response rates among families at different income levels in 1966, there are only very small differences in response rates among occupation and education groups. Response rates are lowest among families headed by laborers and service workers and highest among farmers and farm managers. Virtually no difference exists between the initial sample and the final subsample with respect to the education of the family head. The response rate for those families whose heads had between 0 and 5 grades of education was only five percentage points lower than the rate associated with most highly educated heads.

Many of the differences in response rate observed for the remaining family characteristics included in Appendix Table D-3 can be explained by the probable mobility of the family unit, and the likelihood of being able to successfully follow the unit if a move occurred. Thus, response rates are lower among families with heads under age 25 than among any other age group. The impact of family size on the ease with which people can move may also explain in part the large differences in response rates between units of different sizes. Single member households, being more transient, are difficult to reinterview. Marriage increases the likelihood of being able to reinterview the household. Finally, the addition of children to the family further increases the response rate to the point where families with 4 or more members were half again as likely to be reinterviewed as single member households.

As expected, the difference in response rate between home owners and renters is large. Investments in housing are generally undertaken by families who envision no immediate need or desire to move and consequently such households are considerably easier to reinterview than are renters for whom costs of relocating are less. A response rate of 61 percent was associated with owners, 17 percent points higher than the rate associated with renters.

In line with the above findings, panel losses are more frequent in large metropolitan areas (central cities of 12 largest standard metropolitan sampling areas and cities with a population of 50,000 and more) than in other areas. Only 41 percent of the families initially interviewed in the largest metropolitan areas remained in the panel while 66 percent of the rural families remained.

Response Rates by Initial Attitudes

Household attitudes toward debt use and personal financial progress are as important to psychological economics as income and wealth are to traditional economics. It is of particular interest then to examine whether or not the resultant distribution of families according to the attitudes they hold is comparable between the initial and final sample, or whether panel losses were relatively heavier within some attitudinal groups than within others.

The results presented in Appendix Table D-4 give very much the same impression as that noted in an earlier article by M. Sobol.[2] Families with more optimistic outlooks and who are likely to be somewhat more dynamic have somewhat higher response rates than do less optimistic families. The differences, however, are small and there is no substantial evidence that the attitudes and experiences of the families who remained in the panel to its completion were likely to be very different from those who dropped out or could not be located for one of the three reinterviews.

Panel mortality produced a slight bias in favor of more favorable attitudes toward the use of installment credit in the final panel. However, here again the difference was very slight.

The comparisons made in these last few pages do not eliminate entirely the possibility that the final consumer panel differs from a similarly defined cross-section in subtle ways that could be important for some analyses. However, in general the comparisons presented here do increase our confidence that the panel does represent fairly well the population of primary families whose heads were under age 60 in early 1967.

[2]Marion Gross Sobol, "Panel Mortality and Panel Bias," *Journal of the American Statistical Association,* March, 1959, pp. 52-68.

Appendix Table D-1

COMPARISON OF THE DEMOGRAPHIC COMPOSITION
OF THE 1970 SURVEY OF CONSUMER FINANCES
AND THE FORD FOUNDATION PANEL IN EARLY 1970

(Percentage Distribution)

Demographic Characteristic	1970 Survey of Consumer Finances[1]	1969-1970 Ford Panel
Age of Head		
Under age 35	35	25
35-44	23	26
45-54	25	28
55-62	17	21
Total	100	100
Education of Head		
8 grades or less	17	20
9-11 grades	17	18
12 grades	21	20
12 grades plus vocational training	12	12
College, no degree	18	14
College, bachelor's degree	9	11
College, advanced degree	6	5
Total	100	100
Total Family Income in 1969		
Less than $3,000	8	5
$3,000-4,999	9	7
$5,000-5,999	5	5
$6,000-7,499	11	8
$7,500-8,499	8	7
$8,500-9,999	9	12
$10,000-12,499	16	16
$12-500-14,999	13	15
$15,000-19,999	13	15
$20,000 or more	8	11
Total	100	100

Appendix Table D-1 (con't)

Demographic Characteristic	1970 Survey of Consumer Finances[1]	1969-1970 Ford Panel
Life Cycle Stage of Family Head		
Young, single	9	2
Young, married, no children	8	3
Young, married, youngest child under 6	24	22
Young, married, youngest child 6 or older	12	18
Older, married, children at home	14	20
Older, married, no children at home	17	20
Older, single	8	8
Any age, single with children	8	6
Total	100	100
Race of Head		
White	87	89
Nonwhite	13	11
Total	100	100
Sex of Head		
Male	85	89
Female	15	11
Total	100	100

[1]Excluded from the 1970 Survey of Consumer Finances are all secondary family units and family units whose head was age 63 or older at the time of the interview.

Appendix Table D-2

EDUCATION OF HEAD BY AGE OF HEAD FOR THE 1970 SURVEY OF CONSUMER FINANCES
AND THE FORD FOUNDATION PANEL STUDY

(Percentage Distribution)

Education of Head in early 1970	Age of Head in Early 1970							
	Under age 35		Age 35 to 44		Age 45 to 54		Age 55 to 62	
	1970 SCF	Ford Panel	1970 SCF	Ford Panel	1970 SCF	Ford Panel	1970 SCF	Ford Panel
8 grades or less	6	6	14	12	22	26	39	39
9-11 grades	14	16	18	21	22	18	17	15
12 grades	37	40	35	34	31	29	23	23
College, no degree	26	20	15	15	13	12	11	10
College, degree	17	18	18	18	12	15	10	13
Total	100	100	100	100	100	100	100	100
Number of Families	724	354	486	365	510	414	359	300
Proportion of Families	35	25	23	25	25	29	17	21

Appendix Table D-3

RESPONSE RATES FOR SELECTED DEMOGRAPHIC GROUPS

(Percentage Distribution and Frequencies)

Demographic Characteristic (Early 1967)	Families Who Completed First Interview		Families Who Completed All Interviews		Response Rate
	Number of families	Percent of families	Number of families	Percent of families	
1966 Family Income					
Less than $3,000	258	10	124	9	48
$3,000-4,999	323	12	141	10	44
$5,000-7,499	583	22	307	21	53
$7,500-9,999	552	21	337	23	61
$10,000-14,999	612	23	352	24	57
$15,000 or more	276	11	180	13	65
Occupation of Head					
Professional, technical	321	12	194	13	60
Managers and officials (non-self-employed)	198	8	117	8	59
Self-employed business-men and artisans	162	6	101	7	62
Clerical and sales workers	281	11	144	10	51
Craftsmen and foremen	468	18	267	19	57
Operatives	543	21	292	20	54
Laborers and service workers	294	11	137	10	47
Farmers and farm managers	93	4	62	4	67
Miscellaneous and retired	244	9	127	9	52
Education of Head					
Less than 6 grades	106	4	58	4	55
6-8 grades	418	16	233	16	56
9-11 grades	518	20	252	17	49
Completed high school	504	19	270	19	54
High school plus non-college training	332	13	193	13	58
Some college, no degree	361	14	210	15	58
College, bachelor's degree	241	9	152	11	63
College, advanced degree	116	5	69	5	59
Not ascertained	8	*	4	*	−

Appendix Table D-3 (con't)

Demographic Characteristic (Early 1967)	Families Who Completed First Interview		Families Who Completed All Interviews		Response Rate
	Number of families	Percent of families	Number of families	Percent of families	
Age of Head					
Under 25	214	8	104	7	49
25-34	645	25	361	25	56
35-44	702	27	381	26	54
45-54	721	28	415	29	58
55-59	322	12	180	13	56
Size of Family					
One person	247	9	103	7	42
Two people	591	23	290	20	49
Three people	498	19	277	19	56
Four people	531	20	317	22	60
Five people	359	14	228	16	63
Six or more people	378	15	226	16	60
Place of Residence					
Central city of 12 largest SMSA's	333	13	137	9	41
Other cities of 50,000 and over	560	22	272	19	49
Urban places of 10,000-49,999	452	17	262	18	58
Urban places of 2,500-9,999	579	22	324	23	56
Rural places in an SMSA	138	5	76	5	55
Rural places not in an SMSA	542	21	370	26	68
Home Ownership					
Owner	1604	62	985	68	61
Renter	909	35	402	28	44
Neither owns nor rents	91	3	54	4	59
All Families	2604	100	1441	100	55

---

*Less than one-half of one percent.

Appendix Table D-4

RESPONSE RATE BY REPORTED FREQUENCY OF DEBT USE, DEBT ATTITUDES AND
PAST AND EXPECTED FINANCIAL PROGRESS

(Percentage Distribution and Frequencies)

Response in Early 1967	Families Who Completed First Interview		Families Who Completed All Interviews		Response Rate
	Number of families	Percent of families	Number of families	Percent of families	
Amount of Time since Age 18 Making Installment Payments					
All the time	222	9	132	9	59
Most of the time	734	28	430	30	59
Only for a period	912	35	508	35	56
Hardly ever	561	21	293	20	52
Never	162	6	76	5	44
Don't know; not ascertained	13	1	6	1	–
Debt Attitude[1] Index Score					
Unfavorable attitudes	78	3	33	2	42
(Score of 1)	108	4	52	4	48
(Score of 2)	273	10	134	9	49
(Score of 3)	412	16	231	16	56
(Score of 4)	637	24	376	26	59
(Score of 5)	541	21	306	22	57
(Score of 6)	433	17	243	17	56
Favorable attitudes	122	5	61	4	50
Financially Better or Worse Off than Year Ago					
Better off	1067	41	635	44	59
Same	1027	40	558	39	54
Worse off	471	18	228	16	48
Uncertain, don't know	29	1	11	1	38
Not ascertained	10	*	4	*	–
Expect to be Better or Worse Off Next Year					
Better off	1159	45	643	45	55
Same	1019	39	575	40	56
Worse off	170	7	87	6	51
Uncertain, don't know	246	9	127	9	52
Not ascertained	10	*	4	*	–

Appendix Table D-4 (con't)

Response in Early 1967	Families Who Completed First Interview		Families Who Completed All Interviews		Response Rate
	Number of families	Percent of families	Number of families	Percent of families	
Income Higher or Lower than 4 Years Ago					
Much higher	979	38	578	40	59
A little higher	920	35	516	36	56
About the same	305	12	152	11	50
Lower	323	12	163	11	50
Don't know, not ascertained	77	3	32	2	42
Expect Income to be Higher or Lower in 4 Years					
Much higher	566	22	314	22	55
A little higher	1121	43	632	44	56
About the same	388	15	214	15	55
Lower	131	5	78	5	59
Don't know	395	15	201	14	51
Not ascertained	3	*	2	*	–

---

*Less than one-half of one percent.

[1]At the time of the first interview in early 1967.

Appendix E

INTERVIEW SCHEDULES

Four interview schedules were employed in carrying out the Consumer Panel Study, one for each of the annual interviews. The questionnaire for the final interview only is reproduced here. The questionnaires for Wave I, Wave II, and Wave III are reproduced in the 1967, 1968, and 1969 *Survey of Consumer Finances* monographs, respectively.

The questionnaires for each of the waves of interviewing are very similar. They do differ in some respects, however. At the time of the first interview in early 1967, questions dealing with the ownership of a number of major household durables were asked. In later interviews these questions were dropped. Data on automobiles owned are available for all years, as are estimates of the total value of all cars owned at the time of each interview. Data on financial assets were obtained only in brackets at the time of the first interview. However, these questions were expanded in subsequent years to provide more information about the family portfolio, and data are available for years two through four on all major financial assets.

A number of topics which were dealt with in detail in each of the first three interviews were only asked about in the last interview if some change had taken place. Thus, changes in housing payments and mortgage obligations were only ascertained at the time of the last interview for families who had moved since the time of the third interview, and the family head's occupation was asked about only if there had been some change. In the final questionnaire a number of new questions were added regarding the work history of wives.

For readers who may be interested in using the panel data for their own research, it may be useful to summarize the time structure of the data. Each round of interviewing took place during the first quarter of the year. Most of the information collected were measures of flow variables, such as income, for the previous calendar year, or status variables at the time of the interview.

A few variables measured changes (either directly or by implication) and some measured intended behavior or expected change for the forthcoming 12 months. Thus, for each of the four interviews data are available for (1) flows over the previous calendar year, (2) stocks at the time of the interview, (3) intentions for the next 12 months, and (4) expectations for the next 12 months.

1970 CONSUMER PANEL STUDY

1970 INT _____   PROJECT 45758   January–February 1970

SURVEY RESEARCH CENTER
INSTITUTE FOR SOCIAL RESEARCH
THE UNIVERSITY OF MICHIGAN
ANN ARBOR, MICHIGAN 48106

(Do not write in above space)

1. Interviewer's Label

2. **P S U** _____

3. **Your Interview No.** _____

4. **Date** _____

5. **Length of Interview** _____
(Minutes)

INTERVIEWER: LIST <u>ALL</u> PERSONS, INCLUDING CHILDREN LIVING IN THE DWELLING UNIT, BY THEIR RELATION TO THE HEAD.

6. All persons, by relation or connection to head	7. Sex	8. Age	9. Family Unit No.	10. Indicate Resp. by Check					
									67 INT
									68 INT
									69 INT
1. HEAD OF DWELLING UNIT			1						
2.									
3.						SU			
4.									
5.					O				
6.									
7.						NC			
8.									
9.						MFC			
10.									
11.									

12. Have there been any changes, in the last year, in the <u>number</u> of people in your family living here?

☐ YES   ☐ NO – (TURN TO O. A1)
  ↓

13. What changes? _____ —

A. HOUSING

A1. (INTERVIEWER: SEE COVER SHEET AND CHECK BOX)

> 1. FAMILY HAS NOT MOVED SINCE INTERVIEWED LAST YEAR — (GO TO Q. A15)

> 5. FAMILY AT DIFFERENT ADDRESS THIS YEAR

A2. Do you (FAMILY UNIT) own this (home/apartment), pay rent, or what?

> OWNS OR IS BUYING THIS (HOME/APARTMENT) — (GO TO Q. A6)

> PAYS RENT ON THIS (HOME/APARTMENT) — (GO TO Q. A4)

> NEITHER OWNS NOR RENTS THIS (HOME/APARTMENT)

(IF NEITHER OWNS NOR RENTS)

A3. What arrangement do you have? _____

_____

(TURN TO Q. A22)

(IF RENTS)

A4. About how much rent do you pay a month? $_____ per mo.

A5. Do you rent it furnished or unfurnished?

> 1. FURNISHED   5. UNFURNISHED

(TURN TO Q. A22)

(IF OWNS OR IS BUYING)

IF R LIVES IN MULTIPLE DU STRUCTURE, TRY TO GET VALUE FOR R'S DU ONLY. HOWEVER IF R CAN GIVE YOU ONLY VALUE OF ENTIRE STRUCTURE, BE SURE TO NOTE THAT FIGURE IS FOR WHOLE STRUCTURE.

A6. How much did the house (farm) cost? $_____

A7. Did you own the place you lived in previously?

> 1. YES   5. NO — (GO TO Q. A9)

A7a. Did you sell it when you moved here?

> 1. YES   5. NO — (GO TO Q. A9)

A8. How much did you sell it for (including broker's fees, if any)? $_____

(GO TO Q. A9)

HS ☐   HV ☐☐☐☐☐   HP ☐☐☐   EQ ☐☐☐☐☐

197

(MOVED AND OWNS OR IS BUYING)

A9. Do you have a mortgage on this present property?

YES   NO - (TURN TO Q. A22)

A10. Do you also have a second mortgage?

YES   NO.

	First Mortgage	Second Mortgage
A11. About how much is your present mortgage now?	$	$
A12. How much are your monthly payments?	$	$
A13. How many years will it be before the mortgage is all paid off?	(YEARS)	(YEARS)
A14. What interest rate are you paying on the mortgage?	(PERCENT)	(PERCENT)

(TURN TO Q. A22)

(DID NOT MOVE)

A15. Do you own this (home/apartment), pay rent, or what?

PAYS RENT ON THIS (HOME/APARTMENT) - (TURN TO Q. A22)

NEITHER OWNS NOR RENTS THIS (HOME/APARTMENT) - (TURN TO Q. A22)

OWNS OR IS BUYING THIS (HOME/APARTMENT)

A16. Do you have a mortgage on this present property?

YES   NO - (TURN TO Q. A22)

A17. Do you also have a second mortgage?

YES   NO

	First Mortgage	Second Mortgage
A18. About how much is your present mortgage now?	$	$
A19. How much are your monthly payments?	$	$
A20. How many years will it be before the mortgage is all paid off?	(YEARS)	(YEARS)
A21. What interest rate are you paying on the mortgage?	(PERCENT)	(PERCENT)

TOT MORT | | | | | | TOT PAY | | |

198

(ASK EVERYONE)

A22. Do you expect to buy or build a house for your own year-round use during the next twelve months?

_____

     (IF NO TO Q. A22)

> A22a. How about during the year after that? _____
>
> _____

B. ADDITIONS AND REPAIRS

(ASK EVERYONE)

B1. Did you have any expenses for work done on this (house and lot/apartment) in 1969 – things like upkeep, additions, improvements, or painting and decorating? (FARMERS EXCLUDE FARM BUILDINGS; LANDLORDS -- EXCLUDE INCOME PROPERTY)

YES   NO - (TURN TO Q. B11)

B2. What was done? -- anything else? (ENTER WORK DONE)⟶			
B3. How much did it cost?	\$_____	\$_____	\$_____
B4. Did you borrow or finance any of it?	YES NO ↓ GO TO BOX A	YES NO ↓ GO TO BOX A	YES NO ↓ GO TO BOX A
B5. How much did you borrow or finance?	\$_____	\$_____	\$_____
B6. Do you have anything left to pay?	YES NO ↓ GO TO BOX A	YES NO ↓ GO TO BOX A	YES NO ↓ GO TO BOX A
B7. Is what you owe for it included in the mortgage on your house?	YES ↓ GO TO BOX A NO	YES ↓ GO TO BOX A NO	YES ↓ GO TO BOX A NO
B8. How much are your payments? B9. How many payments do you have left?	\$_____ per_____ _____	\$_____ per_____ _____	\$_____ per_____ _____
B10. How much do you have left to pay?	\$_____	\$_____	\$_____

BOX A   (INTERVIEWER: REPEAT Q'S B3-B10 FOR EACH ADDITION OR REPAIR MENTIONED, THEN TURN TO Q. B11)

TAB   ADD + REP   PAYM   RID

200

(ASK EVERYONE)

B11. Do you expect to make any large expenditures for work on this (house and lot/apartment)
during the next 12 months -- things like upkeep, additions, or improvements, or
painting and decorating? (FARMERS -- EXCLUDE FARM BUILDINGS; LANDLORDS EXCLUDE
INCOME PROPERTY)

| 1. YES | | 3. POSSIBLY, IT DEPENDS | | 5. NO |

C. CARS

C1. This next set of questions is about cars. Altogether, how many people are there in
your family living here who can drive?

_____DRIVERS

C2. Do you or anyone else here in your family own a car?

| YES | | NO | - (TURN TO PAGE 9, Q. C36)

C3. Altogether, how many cars do you and your family living here own? _____CARS

(INTERVIEWER: ASK REST OF PAGE FOR <u>EACH CAR OWNED</u> BY FU)			
Now I'd like to ask a few questions about the car(s) you have now.	CAR #	CAR #	CAR #
C4. What year model is it?	19____	19____	19____
C5. What make of car is it? (2 WORD ANSWER)			
C6. Is it a 2-door sedan, a 4-door sedan, a station wagon, convertible, or what?			
C7. Is it a compact, regular size, something in-between, or what?			
C8. Did you buy this car new or used?	1. NEW 2. USED	1. NEW 2. USED	1. NEW 2. USED
C9. In what year did you buy it?	19____	19____	19____

ASK Q'S C10-C15 <u>FOR EACH CAR</u> BOUGHT IN 1968 OR EARLIER.
ASK Q'S C16-C29 <u>FOR EACH CAR</u> BOUGHT IN 1969 OR 1970.

201

LIST ALL CARS BOUGHT IN 1968 OR EARLIER (FROM Q. C9), AND ASK C10-C15 FOR EACH CAR.

	CAR #	CAR #	CAR #
LIST MODEL YEAR AND MAKE——→			
C10. Do you (R AND FU) owe money on that car now?	5. NO – (GO TO BOX B) 2. YES ↓	5. NO – (GO TO BOX B) 2. YES ↓	5. NO – (GO TO BOX B) 2. YES ↓
C11. How much are your payments?	$_____ per_____	$_____ per_____	$_____ per_____
C12. How many payments do you have left to make?	_____	_____	_____
C13. Will the final payment be the same as the others?	1. SAME (GO TO Q. C15) 5. DIFFERENT ↓	1. SAME (GO TO Q. C15) 5. DIFFERENT ↓	1. SAME (GO TO Q. C15) 5. DIFFERENT ↓
(IF DIFFERENT) C14. Then how much will the final payment be?	$_____	$_____	$_____
C15. Do your car payments include automobile insurance?	1. YES 5. NO	1. YES 5. NO	1. YES 5. NO

BOX B   (INTERVIEWER: ASK QUESTIONS C10-C15 FOR EACH CAR BOUGHT IN 1968 OR EARLIER AND THEN TURN TO NEXT PAGE)

RID   [| | |]   [| | |]   [| | |]

RNID   [| | |]   [| | |]   [| | |]

202

LIST CARS BOUGHT IN 1969 OR 1970 (FROM Q. C9), AND ASK C16-C29 FOR EACH CAR.

Now about the cars you bought in 1969 or already this year --

	CAR #	CAR #	CAR #
LIST MODEL YEAR AND MAKE————————→			
C16. When did you buy this car?	_____ (MON)	_____ (MON)	_____ (MON)
C17. What was the total price of this car?	$_____	$_____	$_____
C18. When you bought this car did you trade-in or sell a car?	1.YES 5.NO	1.YES 5.NO	1.YES 5.NO
(IF TRADE-IN OR SALE) C19. What did you get for the trade-in or sale? TI	$_____	$_____	$_____
C20. How much did you pay down in cash?	$_____	$_____	$_____
C21. Did you borrow or finance part of the total price?	5.NO -(GO TO BOX C) 1.YES	5.NO -(GO TO BOX C) 1.YES	5.NO -(GO TO BOX C) 1.YES
(IF BORROWED) C22. How much did you borrow, not including financing charges? AB	$_____	$_____	$_____
C23. How much are your payments and how often are they made?	$_____ per_____	$_____ per_____	$_____ per_____
C24. How many payments did you agree to make altogether?	_____	_____	_____
C25. How many payments have you made?	_____	_____	_____
C26. How many payments do you have left to make?	_____	_____	_____
C27. Will the final payment be the same as the others?	1.SAME (GO TO Q. C29) 5.DIFFERENT	1.SAME (GO TO Q. C29) 5.DIFFERENT	1.SAME (GO TO Q. C29) 5.DIFFERENT
(IF DIFFERENT) C28. Then how much will the final payment be?	$_____	$_____	$_____
C29. Do your car payments include automobile insurance?	1.YES 5.NO	1.YES 5.NO	1.YES 5.NO

BOX C (INTERVIEWER: ASK QUESTIONS C16-C29 FOR EACH CAR BOUGHT IN 1969 OR 1970, THEN GO TO NEXT PAGE)

RID ☐☐☐☐   ☐☐☐☐   ☐☐☐☐

RNID ☐☐☐☐   ☐☐☐☐   ☐☐☐☐

LIST ALL CARS BOUGHT IN 1969 OR 1970 WITH A TRADE-IN OR SALE ("YES" TO C18)
ASK C30-C35 ABOUT THE TRADE-IN OR SALE.

Now about the car(s) you (traded-in/sold) when you bought your ─────────────▷ (LIST MODEL-YEAR AND MAKE OF CAR BOUGHT)	CAR #	CAR #
C30. What year model was the car you (traded-in/sold)?	19___ (YEAR)	19___ (YEAR)
C31. What make was it? (2 WORD ANSWER)	_____ _____	_____ _____
C32. What year did you buy the car you (traded-in/sold)?	19___ (YEAR)	19___ (YEAR)
C33. Did you buy it new or used?	1. NEW 2. USED	1. NEW 2. USED
C34. Was it a 2-door sedan, a 4-door sedan, station wagon, convertible, or what?	_____	_____
C35. When you (traded it in/sold it) was it in good shape, did it need some repairs, or was something seriously wrong with it?	1. GOOD SHAPE 3. SOME REPAIRS 5. SERIOUSLY WRONG	1. GOOD SHAPE 3. SOME REPAIRS 5. SERIOUSLY WRONG

(ASK EVERYONE)

C36. Speaking now of the automobile market - do you think the next twelve months or so will be a good time or a bad time to buy a car?

| 1. GOOD | 3. PRO-CON | 5. BAD | 8. DON'T KNOW |

C37. Do you people expect to buy a car during the next twelve months or so? _____

_____

C38. Suppose you needed a thousand dollars for a car which you would repay in twelve monthly payments, about how much do you think the interest or carrying charges would be? (IF DEPENDS ON WHERE BORROWED -- ASK FOR SOURCE)

_____

C38a. (IF RESPONDENT GIVES A DOLLAR ANSWER) About how much would that be in percent of what is borrowed?
_____PERCENT

(INTERVIEWER: ENCOURAGE WIFE TO HELP WITH THIS SECTION)

D. OTHER DURABLES

D1. How about large things for the home -- did you buy anything in 1969 such as furniture, a refrigerator, stove, washing machine, color television set, air conditioner, household appliances, and so on?

YES   NO - (GO TO Q. D13)

D2. What did you buy? -- anything else? (ENTER EACH ITEM)————>			
D3. How much did it cost, not counting financing charges?	$_____	$_____	$_____
D4. Was there a trade-in, or did you sell your old one, or what?	NEITHER (GO TO BOX D) TI S	NEITHER (GO TO BOX D) TI S	NEITHER (GO TO BOX D) TI S
(IF TRADE-IN OR SALE) D5. How much did you get for it?	$_____	$_____	$_____
D6. Did you buy it on credit, or pay cash, or what?	CASH ONLY (GO TO BOX D) CREDIT	CASH ONLY (GO TO BOX D) CREDIT	CASH ONLY (GO TO BOX D) CREDIT
D7. How much did you pay down in cash?	$_____	$_____	$_____
D8. Do you still have anything left to pay?	YES NO (GO TO BOX D)	YES NO (GO TO BOX D)	YES NO (GO TO BOX D)
(IF YES TO Q. D8) D9. How much are the payments and how often are they made?	$_____ per_____	$_____ per_____	$_____ per_____
D10. Are the payments all the same amount, or does what you pay depend on how much you owe, or what?	ALL SAME DEPEND ON BALANCE	ALL SAME DEPEND ON BALANCE	ALL SAME DEPEND ON BALANCE
D11. How many more payments do you have left to make?	_____	_____	_____
D12. How much do you have left to pay?	$_____	$_____	$_____
BOX **D** (INTERVIEWER: REPEAT Q'S D3-D12 FOR EACH ITEM MENTIONED, THEN GO TO Q. D13)			

TC	TI	NO	TAB	MP	RID

(ASK EVERYONE)

D13. Now about the big things people buy for their homes -- such as furniture, house furnishings, refrigerator, stove, television, and things like that. Generally speaking, do you think now is a good or a bad time for people to buy major household items?

| 1. GOOD | | 3. PRO-CON | | 5. BAD | | 8. UNCERTAIN |

D14. Do you expect to buy any large items such as furniture, a refrigerator, stove, washing maching, television set, air conditioner, household appliances and so on during the next 12 months?

| 1. YES | | 2. PROBABLY | | 3. MAYBE | | 5. NO | - (GO TO Q. E1)

D14a. What do you expect to buy? _____

E. OTHER MAJOR TRANSACTIONS

E1. Now how about larger recreation and hobby items -- did you buy anything of this sort during 1969 -- for instance, camping equipment, a vacation trailer, photographic equipment, a musical instrument, power tools, a boat, sports equipment, and so on?

| YES | | NO | - (TURN TO Q. E10)

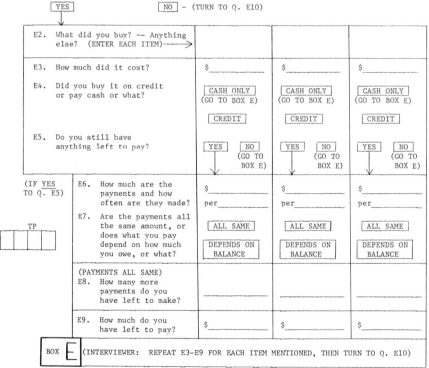

206

E10. Did you or anyone else in the family take a vacation trip of five days or more during the last twelve months?

1. YES   5. NO - (GO TO Q. E13)

E11. Roughly how much did you spend altogether, including transportation and other things that cost more than if you were home?
$_____

E12. Do you owe any money on your vacation expenses?

1. YES   5. NO - (GO TO Q. E13)

(IF STILL OWES, ASK F2-F6 ON NEXT PAGE AND ENTER DETAILS THERE)

E13. Sometimes families are faced with rather unusual or unexpected expenses. During the last year did your family have expenses for illness, accidents or any other unexpected situations?

1. YES   5. NO - (GO TO Q. F1)

E14. What was that? _____

E15. About how much did you spend? $_____

E16. When did you make this expenditure? _____(month)

E17. Do you owe any money for these expenses?   TC [ ][ ][ ][ ]

1. YES   5. NO

(IF STILL OWES, ASK F2-F6 ON NEXT PAGE AND ENTER DETAILS THERE)

F. OTHER PAYMENTS AND DEBT

F1. We've talked about housing, cars, household appliances and various other expenditures. Do you owe for anything else on which you make regular payments?

| 1. YES, OWES | | 5. NO ADDITIONAL DEBT | - (GO TO Q. F7) |

F2. What is it for? (ENTER ITEMS)			
F3. How much did you borrow?	$_____	$_____	$_____
F4. How much are the payments? (IF NO REGULAR PAYMENTS ASK F15 THROUGH F18 FOR THIS ITEM)	$_____	$_____	$_____
F5. How many have you already made?	_____	_____	_____
F6. How many do you have left to make?	_____	_____	_____

F7. Are you currently making payments on a revolving charge account for purchases that we haven't talked about yet?
| YES | - (ENTER DETAILS IN Q. F2-F6) | NO |

F8. How about travel expenses or medical expnses - do you owe for anything like that?
| YES | - (ENTER DETAILS IN Q. F2-F6) | NO |

F9. Do you make (any other) regular payments, say, to a loan or finance company, that we have not yet talked about?
| YES | - (ENTER DETAILS IN Q. F2-F6) | NO |

F10. INTERVIEWER, CHECK ONE: | 1. R HAS MENTIONED MONTHLY PAYMENTS (INCLUDE MORTGAGES) | | 2. R DOES NOT HAVE ANY MONTHLY PAYMENTS (TURN TO Q. F14) |

F11. Suppose you'd like to make some more large purchases; would it be easy or a hardship for you to take care of larger pavments than you make now?

_____

F12. In making payments on your debts in 1969, did you make the payments in the way they were scheduled, did you get behind, or did you make payments that were larger or more frequent than scheduled?

| 1. AS SCHEDULED | | 2. FASTER OR LARGER | | 3. BOTH "GOT BEHIND" AND "FASTER OR LARGER" |

| 4. GOT BEHIND | | 8. D.K. |

F13. Did you reschedule or renegotiate a debt in 1969? | 1. YES | | 5. NO |

208

F14. Do you owe any money on which you don't make regular <u>payments</u>; like a loan on a
life insurance policy, or a debt to some person or bank?

     1. YES   5. NO - (GO TO Q. F19)

F15. What was it used for? (ENTER LOAN)→			
F16. How much do you still owe?	$_____	$_____	$_____
F17. Do you pay interest on it?	1. YES / 5. NO	1. YES / 5. NO	1. YES / 5. NO

F18. Do you have any other loans like that?

      1. YES - (ENTER DETAILS IN Q. F16-F18)   5. NO - (GO TO Q. F19)

      (INTERVIEWER: ASK F16-F18 FOR EACH LOAN MENTIONED)

RNID ☐☐☐☐

F19. In 1969 did you <u>finish</u> making payments on a loan or something you had bought?

     1. YES   5. NO - (GO TO Q. G1)

F20. What was that? (ENTER ITEM)→					
F21. What month did you finish?	(MONTH)	(MONTH)	(MONTH)	(MONTH)	(MONTH)
F22. How much was the loan?	$_____	$_____	$_____	$_____	$_____
F23. Did you start making these payments on (ITEM) in 1969?	1. YES / 5. NO	1. YES / 5. NO	1. YES / 5. NO	1. YES / 5. NO	1. YES / 5. NO

G. GENERAL ATTITUDES

G1. We are interested in how people are getting along financially these days. Would you say that you and your family are better off or worse off financially than you were a year ago?

| 1. BETTER NOW | 3. SAME | 5. WORSE NOW | 8. UNCERTAIN |

G2. Now looking ahead - do you think that a year from now you people will be better off financially, or worse off, or just about the same as now?

| 1. BETTER | 3. SAME | 5. WORSE | 8. UNCERTAIN |

G3. And how about four years from now, do you expect that you and your family will be better off, worse off, or just about the same as now?

| 1. BETTER | 3. SAME | 5. WORSE | 8. UNCERTAIN |

G4. Thinking about prices in general, I mean the prices of the things you buy - do you think they will go up in the next year or so, or go down, or stay where they are now?

| 1. WILL GO UP | 3. STAY THE SAME (GO TO Q. G5) | 5. WILL GO DOWN (GO TO Q. G5) |

G4a. How large a price increase do you expect? Of course nobody can know for sure, but would you say that a year from now prices will be about 1 or 2% higher, or 5%, or closer to 10% higher than now, or what?

G5. Now turning to business conditions in the country as a whole - do you think that during the next twelve months we'll have good times financially, or bad times, or what?

| 1. GOOD TIMES | 2. GOOD, WITH QUALIFICATIONS | 3. PRO-CON |

| 4. BAD, WITH QUALIFICATIONS | 5. BAD TIMES | 8. UNCERTAIN |

G6. Looking ahead, which would you say is more likely - that in the country as a whole we'll have continuous good times during the next five years or so, or that we will have periods of widespread unemployment or depression, or what?

(IF DON'T KNOW OR DEPENDS) G6a. On what does it depend in your opinion?

210

H. OCCUPATION AND EMPLOYMENT

H1. Next we would like to talk with you about your work and the employment of others in the family. How about your present job? Are you (HEAD) working now, unemployed or laid off, retired and not working, or what?

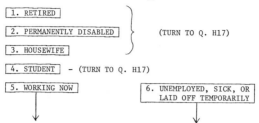

```
1. RETIRED
2. PERMANENTLY DISABLED     (TURN TO Q. H17)
3. HOUSEWIFE
4. STUDENT  - (TURN TO Q. H17)
5. WORKING NOW          6. UNEMPLOYED, SICK, OR
                           LAID OFF TEMPORARILY
```

H2. Have you (HEAD) changed your main occupation since this time last year?

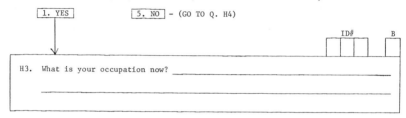

```
1. YES          5. NO  - (GO TO Q. H4)
```

ID#   B

H3. What is your occupation now? _____

_____

H4. Have you (HEAD) changed the business you work in since this time last year?

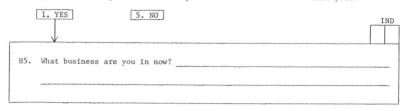

```
1. YES          5. NO
```

IND

H5. What business are you in now? _____

_____

INTERVIEWER: IF YES TO EITHER Q. H2 or Q. H4 ASK Q. H6, OTHERWISE GO TO Q. H7

H6. Do you (HEAD) work for someone else, or yourself, or what?

```
2. SOMEONE ELSE     3. BOTH SOMEONE ELSE AND SELF     1. SELF ONLY
```

211

(INTERVIEWER: ASK H7-H15 FOR HEAD'S MAIN JOB)

H7.   How many weeks of vacation did you (HEAD) actually take in 1969?   _____WEEKS

H8.   How many weeks were you (HEAD) unemployed last year?   _____WEEKS

H9.   How many weeks were you (HEAD) ill or not working for any
       other reason last year?   _____WEEKS

H10.   Then, how many weeks did you (HEAD) actually work on the
       job in 1969?   _____WEEKS

H11.   How many hours a weeks did you (HEAD) usually work when
       you were working on your main job?   _____HRS/WK

H12.   Did you (HEAD) also have a second job in 1969?

        1. YES   5. NO - (GO TO Q. H13)
          ↓

       H12a.   About how many hours altogether did you (HEAD)
               work in 1969 on an extra job?   _____HOURS

H13.   Some people would like to work more hours a week on their (main) job if they
       could make more money that way. Others would prefer to work fewer hours a
       week even if they earned less. How do you feel about this?

        1. MORE   5. FEWER   3. SAME   8. DON'T KNOW

H14.   On the job that you have now (that is your main job) could you work more hours
       and get paid for them if you wanted to?

        1. YES, COULD WORK MORE HOURS

        5. NO, COULD NOT WORK MORE HOURS

H15.   If for some reason you wanted to work fewer hours on the (main) job that you
       have now, could you arrange to do this?

        1. YES, COULD WORK FEWER HOURS

        5. NO, COULD NOT WORK FEWER HOURS

H16.   Would you consider it a hardship if you had to work more hours than you work now
       to make ends meet?

        1. YES

        5. NO

        OTHER (please specify) _____

212

H17. (INTERVIEWER: CHECK BOX)

| MALE FU HEAD HAS WIFE | | MALE FU HEAD HAS NO WIFE | (TURN TO Q. J1) | | FEMALE HEAD | (TURN TO Q. J1) |

H18. Did your wife do any work for money during 1969?

1. YES   5. NO - (GO TO Q. H23)   B

H19. What kind of work did she do? _____

H20. Was she working for someone else, herself, or what?

2. SOMEONE ELSE   3. BOTH SOMEONE ELSE AND SELF   1. SELF

H21. About how many hours a week did she usually work when she was working?

_____

H22. How many weeks did she actually work in 1969? _____

(GO TO Q. H25)

H23. Has your wife worked anytime during the last 2 years?

5. NO   1. YES - (GO TO Q. H25)

H24. About how many years ago did your wife last hold a job?

_____YEARS AGO

H25. Since you and your wife have been married, has your wife held a job more than half of the time or less than half of the time?

    | MORE THAN HALF OF THE TIME | - (GO TO Q. H25b)

    | LESS THAN HALF OF THE TIME |
                ↓

H25a. Has she held a job just about half of the time, or about one-quarter of the time, or less than one-quarter of the time?

    _____ (TURN TO Q. J1)

H25b. Has she held a job just about half the time, or closer to three-quarters of the time, or more than three-quarters of the time?

    _____

J. CHILDRENS EDUCATION

J1. We are interested in your children's education. Do you have any children in college now?

| 1. YES | | 5. NO | - (GO TO Q. J2)

J1a. About how much money do you contribute to their support each year? $_____

J2. (INTERVIEWER: SEE FACE SHEET AND CHECK ONE)

| NO CHILDREN 14 OR OLDER | - (GO TO Q. K1)

| ONE OR MORE CHILDREN 14 OR OLDER |

J3. Do you have any children who will start college sometime during the next three years?

| 1. YES | | 3. MAY (HOPE WILL) GO TO COLLEGE | | 5. NO | - (GO TO Q. K1)

J4. How many children is that? _____

J5. How do you expect the college education to be paid for?

_____

_____

J5a. (IF VAGUE ANSWER OR ONLY SAYS THE FAMILY WILL PAY FOR IT ASK:)
Where will the money come from?

_____

_____

J6. Have you set aside any money to pay for (his/their) college education?

| 1. YES | | 5. NO |

J7. About how much do you think it will cost you each year for a child who is attending college?

$_____

K. INCOME

K1. In this survey of families all over the country, we are trying to get an accurate
picture of people's financial situation.

(INTERVIEWER: ASK IF NECESSARY AND CHECK ONE)

| 1. FARMER (AS MAIN JOB) | | NOT FARMER (GO TO Q. K5) |

K2. What were your total receipts from farming in 1968,
including soil bank payments and commodity credit loans? $_____ (A)

K3. What were your total operating expenses,
not counting living expenses? $_____ (B)

K4. That left you a net income from farming of (A - B) ...
is that right? $_____

(ASK EVERYONE)

K5. Did you or anyone else in the family living here own a business at any time in 1969,
or have a financial interest in any business enterprise?

| YES | | NO | - (TURN TO Q. K10)

K6. What kind of business is it? _____

_____

K7. Is it a corporation or an unincorporated business or do you have an interest
in both kinds?

| CORPORATION | - (TURN TO Q. K10)

| UNINCORPORATED | | BOTH | | DON'T KNOW |

K8. How much was your (family's) share of the total income
from the business in 1969 -- that is, the amount you
took out plus any profit left in? $_____

K9. About how much would you say that your (FU) share of
the business is worth -- I mean what would you get out
of it if it were sold and all the debts paid off? $_____

K10. How much did you (HEAD) receive from wages and salaries in 1969, that is, before anything was deducted for taxes or other things? $_____

K11. In addition to this, did you (HEAD) have any income from overtime, bonuses, or commissions?

| YES | | NO | - (GO TO Q. K12) |

K11a. How much was that? $_____

K12. Did you (HEAD) receive any other income in 1969 from:

(IF YES TO ANY ITEM, ASK, "How much was it?" AND ENTER AMOUNT AT RIGHT)

(IF NO, ENTER "0")

NOTE: SHOW CALCULATIONS, IF ANY

a. professional practice or trade . . . . $_____

b. farming or market gardening, roomers or boarders . . . . $_____

c. dividends . . . . $_____

d. interest, trust funds, royalties, or rent . . . . $_____

e. social security . . . . $_____

f. other retirement pay, pensions, or annuities . . . . $_____

g. any other sources, like family allotments, unemployment compensation, welfare, or help from relatives . . . . $_____

h. anything else _____ $_____
                    (SPECIFY)

(INTERVIEWER: CHECK BOX)

K13. | MALE FU HEAD HAS WIFE | | MALE FU HEAD HAS NO WIFE | | FEMALE FU HEAD |
                                  (GO TO Q. K17)   (GO TO Q. K17)

K14. Did your wife have any income during 1969?

| YES | | NO | - (GO TO Q. K17)

K15. Was it income from wages, a business, or what? Any other income?

_____   _____
(SOURCE)   (SOURCE)

K16. How much was it before deductions? $_____ + $_____ = $_____

217

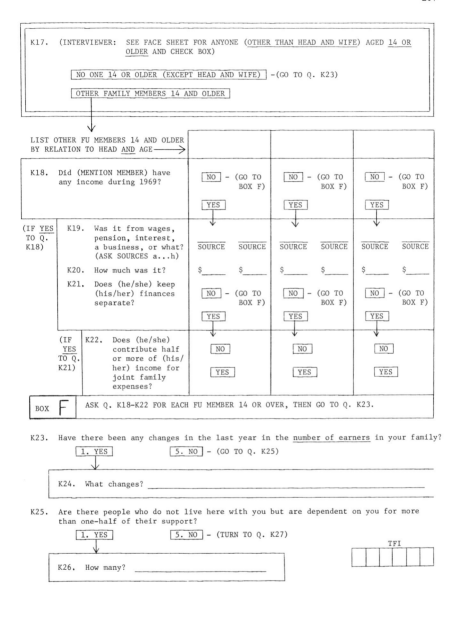

K17. (INTERVIEWER: SEE FACE SHEET FOR ANYONE (OTHER THAN HEAD AND WIFE) AGED 14 OR OLDER AND CHECK BOX)

| NO ONE 14 OR OLDER (EXCEPT HEAD AND WIFE) | –(GO TO Q. K23)

| OTHER FAMILY MEMBERS 14 AND OLDER |

LIST OTHER FU MEMBERS 14 AND OLDER BY RELATION TO HEAD AND AGE ⟶

K18. Did (MENTION MEMBER) have any income during 1969?

| NO | – (GO TO BOX F)   YES

| NO | – (GO TO BOX F)   YES

| NO | – (GO TO BOX F)   YES

(IF YES TO Q. K18)

K19. Was it from wages, pension, interest, a business, or what? (ASK SOURCES a...h)

SOURCE   SOURCE

K20. How much was it? $____ $____

K21. Does (he/she) keep (his/her) finances separate? | NO | – (GO TO BOX F)   YES

| NO | – (GO TO BOX F)   YES

| NO | – (GO TO BOX F)   YES

(IF YES TO Q. K21)

K22. Does (he/she) contribute half or more of (his/her) income for joint family expenses?

| NO | | YES |

| NO | | YES |

| NO | | YES |

BOX F   ASK Q. K18–K22 FOR EACH FU MEMBER 14 OR OVER, THEN GO TO Q. K23.

K23. Have there been any changes in the last year in the number of earners in your family?
| 1. YES | | 5. NO | – (GO TO Q. K25)

K24. What changes? _____

K25. Are there people who do not live here with you but are dependent on you for more than one-half of their support?
| 1. YES | | 5. NO | – (TURN TO Q. K27)

K26. How many? _____

TFI

218

K27. Was your family's total income higher in 1969 than it was the year before that (1968), or lower, or what?

| HIGHER IN 1969 | | LOWER IN 1969 | | SAME | - (GO TO Q. K30)

K28. What are the main reasons why it was (higher/lower)? _____

_____

K29. Was it a lot (higher/lower) or just a little (higher/lower)?

| A LOT | | A LITTLE |

K30. Thinking back to what your family income was about four years ago, say for 1966, are you making much more now, a little more, the same, or less?

| 1. MUCH MORE | | 2. A LITTLE MORE | | 3. THE SAME | | 5. LESS |

K31. How do you think your total family income for this year, 1970, will compare with the past year, 1969 - will it be much higher, a little higher, about the same, or lower?

| 1. 1970 MUCH HIGHER | | 2. 1970 A LITTLE HIGHER | | 3. ABOUT THE SAME | | 4. 1970 LOWER |

K32. Thinking ahead about four years, would you say that your family income will be much higher, a little higher, the same, or smaller than it is now?

| 1. MUCH HIGHER | | 2. A LITTLE HIGHER | | 3. THE SAME | | 5. SMALLER | | 8. D.K. |

K33. If your family needed more money because of reduced income or unusual expenses, are there ways you could get the extra money by working more hours, through extra jobs, by changing your job, or by someone else in the family going to work?

| YES | | 0. NO | - (GO TO Q. K34)

K33a. How could you get the extra money?

NOTE: CHECK AS MANY AS APPLY

| 1. COULD WORK MORE HOURS |

| 2. COULD TAKE EXTRA JOB |

| 3. COULD CHANGE JOBS |

| SOMEONE ELSE IN FAMILY COULD GO TO WORK |

Who could work? | 4. WIFE | | 5. SOMEONE ELSE |

| OTHER | (specify)_____

K34. Suppose a family has children but they are all in school -- would you say it is a good thing for the wife to take a job, or a bad thing, or what?

_____

L. ATTITUDES

We're interested in how people feel about making payments on things, for instance when they buy on time, or borrow.

L1. Do you (HEAD) think it is a good idea or a bad idea for people to buy things on the installment plan?

_____

    L2. Why do you think so? _____

_____

L3. People have many different reasons for borrowing money which they pay back over a period of time.

Would you say it is all right for someone like yourself to borrow money . . .

a) to cover expenses due to illness	1. YES	5. NO
b) to cover the expenses of a vacation trip	1. YES	5. NO
c) to finance the purchase of a fur coat or jewelry	1. YES	5. NO
d) to cover living expenses when income is cut	1. YES	5. NO
e) to finance educational expenses	1. YES	5. NO
f) to finance the purchase of a car	1. YES	5. NO
g) to finance the purchase of furniture	1. YES	5. NO
h) to pay bills which have piled up	1. YES	5. NO

L4. Mr. Smith has just bought a car on time although he has enough money in the bank to pay cash. Why do you think he bought the car on time?

_____

_____

    L4a. What kind of a man do you think he is? _____

_____

220

L5. Since you (HEAD) were in your 20's how much of the time have you been making installment payments on something or other; all the time, most of the time, only for a period of time, or hardly ever?

| ALL THE TIME | MOST OF THE TIME | ONLY FOR A PERIOD | HARDLY EVER | NEVER (GO TO Q. L12) |

L6. We are interested in how creditors treat the people they give credit to. Has anyone ever refused to give you credit you needed to make a large purchase, that is for something that cost $100 or more?

    1. YES   5. NO

L7. Have you ever wanted to open a charge account and been told that you couldn't?

    1. YES   5. NO - (GO TO Q. L8)

    L7a. What reason were you given? _____

    _____

L8. Has anyone ever threatened you with repossession of something you bought on credit?

    1. YES   5. NO

L9. Has a creditor ever turned your bill over to a collection agency?

    1. YES   5. NO

L10. Have you ever been told by a creditor that your wages might be garnisheed, that is did anyone ever say they could have your employer take money out of your pay check if you didn't pay a bill?

    1. YES   5. NO

L11. (IF R ANSWERS YES TO ONE OR MORE OF Q. L8-L10) When creditors have tried to give you a hard time has it been over a small amount, say, less than $100 or over something larger? _____

    _____

(ASK EVERYONE)
L12. Do you know whether you have a credit rating?

    YES   NO - (GO TO Q. M1)

    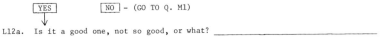
    L12a. Is it a good one, not so good, or what? _____

    _____

M. ASSETS

M1. Do you or others in your family now carry any life insurance which you purchased
yourself or which your employer provides as part of employment benefits?

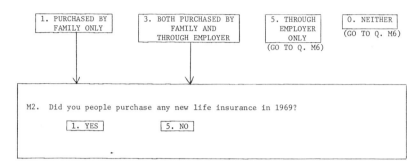

```
┌──────────────────┐   ┌──────────────────┐   ┌──────────────┐   ┌──────────────┐
│ 1. PURCHASED BY  │   │ 3. BOTH PURCHASED BY │  │ 5. THROUGH  │   │ 0. NEITHER   │
│    FAMILY ONLY   │   │    FAMILY AND     │   │   EMPLOYER   │   └──────────────┘
└──────────────────┘   │  THROUGH EMPLOYER │   │    ONLY      │   (GO TO Q. M6)
                       └──────────────────┘   └──────────────┘
                                              (GO TO Q. M6)
```

M2. Did you people purchase any new life insurance in 1969?

1. YES   5. NO

M6. Do you (R AND FU) have any certificates of deposit or savings certificates?

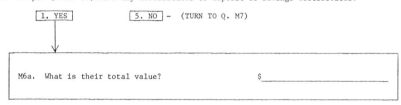

1. YES   5. NO - (TURN TO Q. M7)

M6a. What is their total value? $_____

222

M7. Do you or others in your family now have any savings accounts at banks, savings and loan associations, or credit unions? (CHECK WHICH APPLY)

| BANK | | SAVINGS AND LOAN ASSN. | | CREDIT UNION | | NO | - (GO TO Q. M11)

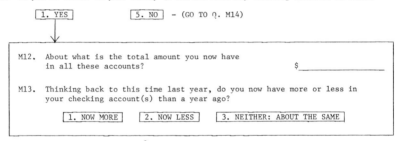

M8. How many accounts do you (FU) have? _____

M9. (Excluding your certificates of deposit) about what is the total amount you have in all these accounts? $_____

M10. Thinking back to this time last year, has the amount in all your (FU's) savings accounts gone up or gone down?

| 1. GONE UP | | 2. GONE DOWN | | 3. NEITHER: STAYED THE SAME |

M11. Do you or others in your family (R AND FU) have any checking accounts at banks?

| 1. YES | | 5. NO | - (GO TO Q. M14)

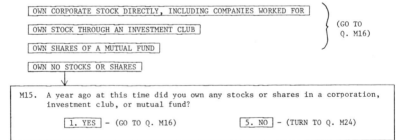

M12. About what is the total amount you now have in all these accounts? $_____

M13. Thinking back to this time last year, do you now have more or less in your checking account(s) than a year ago?

| 1. NOW MORE | | 2. NOW LESS | | 3. NEITHER: ABOUT THE SAME |

(ASK EVERYONE)
M14. Do you (R AND FU) own any common or preferred stock in a corporation, including companies you have worked for, or own stock through an investment club, or own shares of a mutual fund? (CHECK THE APPROPRIATE BOXES)

| OWN CORPORATE STOCK DIRECTLY, INCLUDING COMPANIES WORKED FOR |

| OWN STOCK THROUGH AN INVESTMENT CLUB | } (GO TO Q. M16)

| OWN SHARES OF A MUTUAL FUND |

| OWN NO STOCKS OR SHARES |

M15. A year ago at this time did you own any stocks or shares in a corporation, investment club, or mutual fund?

| 1. YES | - (GO TO Q. M16) | 5. NO | - (TURN TO Q. M24)

223

(IF OWNS STOCK OR MUTUAL FUND SHARES)

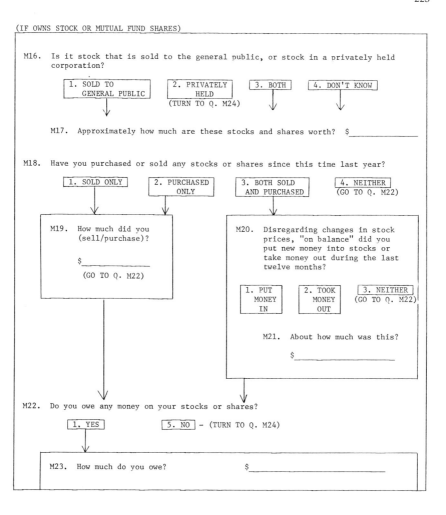

M16. Is it stock that is sold to the general public, or stock in a privately held corporation?

1. SOLD TO GENERAL PUBLIC
2. PRIVATELY HELD (TURN TO Q. M24)
3. BOTH
4. DON'T KNOW

M17. Approximately how much are these stocks and shares worth? $_____

M18. Have you purchased or sold any stocks or shares since this time last year?

1. SOLD ONLY
2. PURCHASED ONLY
3. BOTH SOLD AND PURCHASED
4. NEITHER (GO TO Q. M22)

M19. How much did you (sell/purchase)?

$_____

(GO TO Q. M22)

M20. Disregarding changes in stock prices, "on balance" did you put new money into stocks or take money out during the last twelve months?

1. PUT MONEY IN
2. TOOK MONEY OUT
3. NEITHER (GO TO Q. M22)

M21. About how much was this?

$_____

M22. Do you owe any money on your stocks or shares?

1. YES
5. NO - (TURN TO Q. M24)

M23. How much do you owe? $_____

M24. Do you (R AND FU) have any government savings bonds, other government bonds, municipal or corporate bonds?

| YES, OWNS BONDS | | DOES NOT OWN BONDS | - (GO TO Q. M27) |

M25. About what is the face value of your bonds altogether? $_____

M26. Thinking back to this time a year ago, do you now have more or less invested in bonds than a year ago?

| 1. NOW MORE | | 2. NOW LESS | | 3. THE SAME |

M27. Did you buy any real estate (other than this place here) such as a lot, summer home, an apartment building, or business property in 1969 or already this year?   (INCLUDE LAND CONTRACTS OR MORTGAGES OWED TO ANY FAMILY MEMBER.)

| 1. YES | | 5. NO | - (GO TO Q. M32)   COR [ ][ ][ ][ ][ ][ ]

M28.	What did you buy? (ENTER PROPERTY BOUGHT) ————————>			
M29.	About how much is it worth?	$_____	$_____	$_____
M30.	Did you borrow any money to make this purchase?	YES NO (SEE BOX G)	YES NO (SEE BOX G)	YES NO (SEE BOX G)
M31.	How much, altogether, did you borrow?	$_____ (SEE BOX G)	$_____ (SEE BOX G)	$_____ (SEE BOX G)

BOX **G**   INTERVIEWER: ASK M29–M31 FOR EACH PROPERTY BOUGHT IN 1969 OR LATER THEN GO TO M32.

(ASK EVERYONE)

M32. Do you owe any money on property which you bought before 1969 (other than the mortgage on this place here)?

| 1. YES | | 5. NO | - (GO TO Q. M33)

M32a. How much do you still owe (not counting debt on property purchased in 1969)? $_____

M33. Have you inherited any money, stocks, bonds, or property since this time last year?

| 1. YES | | 5. NO | - (GO TO Q. M34)

> M33a. What was the inheritance worth? $_____

M34. (INTERVIEWER: DOES FAMILY HAVE CHECKING ACCOUNTS, SAVINGS ACCOUNTS, STOCKS, AND BONDS?)

| FU HAS NONE OF THE ABOVE | - (GO TO Q. M37)

| FU HAS ONE OR MORE OF THE ABOVE |

M35. Considering all your reserve funds that we've discussed, "on balance", did you put money into or take money out in the last year?

| 1. PUT MONEY IN | | 2. TOOK MONEY OUT | | 3. NEITHER, STAYED THE SAME | (GO TO Q. M37)

M36. Is this an unusually large (increase/decrease), or is it rather typical?

| 1. UNUSUALLY LARGE | | 2. RATHER TYPICAL |

(ASK EVERYONE)
M37. Are you (HEAD) married, single, widowed, divorced, or separated?

| 1. MARRIED | | 2. SINGLE | | 3. WIDOWED | | 4. DIVORCED | | 5. SEPARATED |

> M37a. How long have you been married?   _____YEARS

M38. Where did you (HEAD) grow up? _____
                                  (STATE if U.S., country if foreign)

M39. Was that on a farm, in a small town, in a city, or what?

| 1. FARM | | 2. SMALL TOWN | | 3. CITY | | OTHER | (specify)_____

L. OBSERVATION DATA

(INTERVIEWER: BY OBSERVATION ONLY)

N1. Sex of <u>Head</u> of Family Unit: ☐ MALE ☐ FEMALE

N2. Sex of Respondent: ☐ MALE ☐ FEMALE

N3. Race: ☐ WHITE ☐ NEGRO ☐ OTHER (specify)_____

N4. Number of calls: _____

N5. Who was present during interview: _____

N6. TYPE OF STRUCTURE IN WHICH FAMILY LIVES:

☐ TRAILER
☐ DETACHED SINGLE FAMILY HOUSE
☐ 2-FAMILY HOUSE, 2 UNITS SIDE BY SIDE
☐ 2-FAMILY HOUSE, 2 UNITS ONE ABOVE
    THE OTHER
☐ DETACHED 3-4 FAMILY HOUSE
☐ ROW HOUSE (3 OR MORE UNITS IN AN
    ATTACHED ROW)

☐ APARTMENT HOUSE (5 OR MORE UNITS,
    3 STORIES OR LESS)
☐ APARTMENT HOUSE (5 OR MORE UNITS,
    4 STORIES OR MORE)
☐ APARTMENT IN A PARTLY COMMERCIAL
    STRUCTURE
☐ OTHER (specify)_____

N7. If Respondent's answers to factual questions (house value, income, etc.) seem
    badly out of line with your observations, please note below.

_____

_____

_____

THUMBNAIL SKETCH

Appendix F

LIST OF TABLES AND GRAPHS